Physical Characteristics of the Spanish Water Dog

(from the Fédération Cynologique Internationale's breed standard)

Body: Robust. *Topline:* Straight. *Withers:* Hardly marked. *Back:* Straight and power *Croup:* Slightly tucked up. *Chest:* Broad and well let down; ribs well arched; diamet of thorax ample, indicating considerable respiratory capacity.

Tail: Set at medium height. Docking must be done at the height of the second to the fourth vertebra.

Hindquarters: Perfectly straight with not too pronounced angulations. *Upper thighs:* Long and well muscled. *Second thighs:* Well developed. *Hock joint:* Well let down. *Hock:* Short, lean and perpendicular to the ground. *Hind feet:* As the forefeet.

Coat: *Hair:* Always curly and of woolly texture. Curly when short, can form cords when long. The recommended maximum length of the hair for shows is 12 cm (15 cm extending the curl) and the minimum is 3 cm to see the quality of the curl.

Color: *Solid:* White, black and chestnut in different shades. *Bicolor:* White and black or white and brown in different shades.

Spanish Water Dog

◆

By Cristina Désarnaud

Contents

Health Care of Your Spanish Water Dog 103

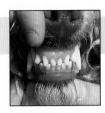

Discover how to select a qualified vet and care for your dog at all stages of life. Topics include vaccinations, skin problems, dealing with external and internal parasites and common medical and behavioral conditions.

Your Senior Spanish Water Dog 132

Consider the care of your senior Spanish Water Dog, including the proper diet for a senior. Recognize the signs of an aging dog, both behavioral and medical; implement a special-care program with your vet and become comfortable with making the final decisions and arrangements for your senior Spanish Water Dog.

Showing Your Spanish Water Dog 139

Experience the dog show world in the conformation ring and beyond. Learn about conformation dog shows as well as obedience, agility and herding trials. Also learn about the FCI, the world's international kennel club.

Behavior of Your Spanish Water Dog 147

Learn to recognize and handle behavioral problems that may arise with your Spanish Water Dog. Topics discussed include separation anxiety, aggression, barking, chewing, digging, begging, jumping up, etc.

KENNEL CLUB BOOKS: **SPANISH WATER DOG**
ISBN: 1-59378-344-2

Photographs by Isabelle Français and Carol Ann Johnson, with additional photographs by: Norvia Behling, T. J. Calhoun, Carolina Biological Supply, David Dalton, Doskocil, James Hayden-Yoav, James R. Hayden, RBP, Bill Jonas, Dwight R. Kuhn, Dr. Dennis Kunkel, Marcelino Pozo, Mikki Pet Products, Phototake, Jean Claude Revy, Dr. Andrew Spielman, Karen Taylor and Alice van Kempen.

Illustrations by Patricia Peters.

The owner would like to thank Inge Fischer, Maria Jose Suarez Moreno, Jaime Veral Pamarch, Diane Philipson and the rest of the owners of the dogs featured in the book.

To my husband, Chema Sanmillan, with all my love.

Although "new" to dog fanciers, the Spanish Water Dog is an ancient breed of Spain, celebrated for its working and swimming abilities, superior intelligence, friendly demeanor and, of course, its eye-catching coat worn in cords or curls.

SPAIN

HISTORY OF THE
SPANISH WATER DOG

Although the Spanish Water Dog's origins trace back many centuries, for the purpose of this discussion of the breed's history, we will focus on some recent events that mark the breed's acceptance into the modern world of pure-bred dogs. It was only in the early 1980s that the world's major kennel clubs finally recognized these remarkable dogs, beginning with the Fédération Cynologique Internationale, the National Kennel Club and the Spanish Royal Canine Society. Currently, the American Kennel Club, The Kennel Club of England and the Canadian Kennel Club have yet to officially accept the breed for registration.

RECOGNITION OF THE BREED

The Spanish Water Dog, or Perro de Agua Español, was officially recognized in Spain during the celebration of the First National Dog Show held in San Pedro de Alcántara in Malaga on May 24, 1981. That day, a cinnamon-colored male owned by Mr. and Mrs. de Klaas Mesdag of Holland was presented and won acclaim. This Dutch family also bred

Spanish Ch. Bartolo de Caba Aramar is just one of the many Spanish Water Dogs being shown throughout Europe, where the breed is enjoying a much-deserved renaissance.

horses, and their contribution to the Perro de Agua was critical to the recognition of the breed.

At the time, the breed was still known as *Turcos Andaluces* (Turkish Andalusians), a name that some dog experts still consider to be more appropriate and perhaps more genuine, since it alludes to the breed's likely true origins. The presentation of the breed resulted through the efforts of a group of aficionados who had researched the background of the *Turcos Andaluces*. Their efforts, along with a few articles that were published in the major dog magazines in Spain, succeeded in promoting the breed within the national and international dog communities.

Veterinarian Andrés Flores, Jose V. García and María Victoria Mañas became the leaders in this campaign to recognize the breed. Other important figures include Antonio García, president of the Spanish association of the breed (AEPDAE); Klaas Mesdag; Santiago Montesinos, the first president of the AEPDAE; David Salamanca, then a member of the Commission for the Spanish Breeds of the Spanish Kennel Club [*Real Sociedad Canina de España* (RSCE)]; Carlos Salas; Jesús Vadillo, then President of the Iberian Environmental Society

Named for the water, this breed enjoys nothing more than to dive in and go for a dip! Unlike most other breeds of dog, the Spanish Water Dog will dive under the water and begin swimming.

Spanish Ch.
Limon, exhibiting
the intelligent
gaze and the
characteristic
corded coat for
which the breed
is prized.

A full profile view of Spanish Ch. Limon shows the unique body outline of the breed.

[*Sociedad Ecologista Ibérica para la Protección de las razas Caninas de Perros de Pastoreo y su Entorno Cultural* (SEIPPEC)]; and many others. We must also recognize the contributions of the many shepherds and goat keepers who allowed dog experts to display their dogs wherever necessary so that others could get to know the characteristics of the breed.

Today, nobody questions Antonio García's incredible personal involvement in the Perro de Agua breed. Some refer to him as "Antonio de Ubrique" because he was born in Ubrique, Cadiz, where he continues to work on promoting the breed. His work has been indispensable in reviving the breed, drafting the first official standard and campaigning the breed to official recognition.

IMPORTANT MODERN HISTORY
On May 14, 1983, the Iberian Environmental Society organized the first show for local shepherd dogs in Plasencia. The SEIPPEC works to promote all matters related to the cattle-raising community in the Iberian Peninsula. Many dogs from that

area were brought forward to participate in this first show, the "Contest of Iberian Shepherd Dogs," which was sponsored by the RSCE. The organization even offered a cash prize to stir up interest in the event, which attracted a number of Perros de Agua Españoles.

The following year, on October 6, 1984, SEIPPEC organized the second show and, again, many Spanish Water Dogs competed. The event was very effective in promoting the breed in Spain. The third year, the show took place on September 28, 1985 and was held in a small village near Madrid called Griñón. The winners of the event were the bitch Trini, bred by Dr. Flores and owned by María Teresa Rupérez, secretary of the SEIPPEC; and the dog Silvestre, owned by Jesús Ruiz. In fact, Trini was the first dog to obtain a *Certificat d'Aptitude au Championnat* (CAC) and, in about a year's time, she earned all of the CACs required to become the first Spanish Champion of the breed.

Yet, when discussing the history of the breed, it is worth noting that the SEIPPEC and the RSCE did not see eye-to-eye about the breed for a period of two years between 1984 and 1986. This happened because, during that time, the SEIPPEC did not agree with some of the demands that the RSCE placed on its breeds and

therefore did not support all of the organization's events. Thus, at the International Exhibition in Madrid in the fall of 1985, only one Spanish Water Dog was entered. However, several months prior, in May of the same year, more than 40 Spanish Water Dogs had been enrolled in the Spanish stud book. Most of these dogs came from Cadiz and Malaga, while five came from Santander.

A key date in the breed's modern history is May 19, 1985, when the RSCE, led by Valentín Álvarez, officially recognized the breed as the Perro de Aqua Español. In that same month, the Fédération Cynologique Internationale (FCI) provisionally registered the breed with the number 336, based on the first standard written for the breed. The model for the standard was a black and white Spanish Water Dog named Lucky, owned by Antonio Moreno.

On September 20 of the following year, 1986, the first breed specialty show was held in Ubrique. This important event was presided over by judge Marqués de Perales, and over 20 dogs competed, 13 of which were owned by Antonio García (with the "de Ubrique" prefix), recognized by everyone as the "father of the breed." Márquez won Best in Show, Nieve de Ubrique was selected as Best Young Dog and Gastor de Ubrique

Consistency of type, the woolly coat texture, a cheerful disposition and a love of water are some of the defining traits of this unique and up-and-coming rare breed.

was named Best Puppy.

It was not until nearly 15 years later that the Spanish Water Dog won international recognition at the FCI's Annual Assembly held in Mexico in June 1999. The breed was thus eligible to compete for *Certificats d'Aptitude au Championnat Internationale de Beauté* (CACIBs) at FCI shows. These certificates are required in order for dogs to become FCI International Champions. The first Spanish Water Dog to win a CACIB was Ch. Cheto de La Galea, a spectacular brown dog owned by Fernando Gutiérrez. This dog won not only the first CACIB for the breed but also three consecutive World Winner titles and, later, his fourth World Champion title, in the year 2000 (the first was in Puerto Rico, the second in Finland, the third in Mexico and the fourth in Italy). He also holds the breed record for most World Champion titles, CACs, CACIBs and Bests in Show, including two at specialty shows in Spain.

The years that have gone by since the mid-1970s, when Mr. Mesdag showed Dr. Flores and

Ms. Mañas how a group of Spanish Water Dogs drove a flock of nearly 800 sheep throughout Moron de la Frontera in Seville, have not been in vain, nor have the efforts of shepherds, goat keepers, sailors and hunters in maintaining the breed as pure as possible. Through the years, and with much effort and special personal commitment, they have managed to avoid mating the breed with others, something that has often negatively affected dogs in the Peninsula.

In recent years, the number of breeders and fanciers has increased all over Spain, and what is more surprising is that the breed has unexpectedly begun to win prestige outside national borders. Today, there are thousands of active prefixes within and outside Spain, as there are hundreds of fanciers who keep and/or breed these dogs. Countries that are far different than and quite distant from Spain, such as Great Britain, Germany and Finland, and even as far away as the United States, have welcomed the Spanish Water Dog. The breed has adjusted perfectly in many countries, which speaks well of its extraordinary capacity to fit in wherever welcomed.

The breed began the 21st century with some impressive numbers entered in the 15th annual specialty show. Whereas the first show in 1986 only attracted 20 dogs, this show in April 2000 attracted 150 dogs. The show was held once again in Ubrique, and Antonio García and Francisco Gómez served as judges. To show how well the breed has progressed in recent years, it is noteworthy that many of the dogs entered were graded "Excellent" by the judges. The bitches' average quality was very high, proven by the 21 "Excellents" that were granted in the Open Bitch Class, which speaks well of the quality of future generations. We should not forget that, not long ago, bitches were relegated to a secondary position in Spain, no matter how absurd this may seem to the dedicated fancier and expert breeder.

At the specialty show in 2000, prefixes such as d'Antrilles, de los Cadetes, Domus, de la Galea, de Palaciego, de la Petaca, de Polvorín, Sierra Alhamillas and de Ubrique were the most well known for their numbers of dogs participating and the scores that they won in the different classes. The top winners in the show were: (Best in Show) Uno de los Cadetes, owned by Pedro Domínguez; (Best Young Dog) Unkas d'Antrilles, owned by Montserrat Rovira; and (Best Puppy) Cheta de la Galea, owned by Fernando Gutiérrez.

At another important event at the turn of the 21st century, the

National Specialty Show for Spanish Breeds, held on September 24, 2000, the Spanish Water Dog made a splashing showing, with 44 dogs entered. The show, for the fourth consecutive year, was sponsored by the Spanish Kennel Club, and the breed judge was José María Piñeiro. Among the Spanish Water Dog winners were: (Best Puppy) Brezu del Llabanazu; (Best Young Dog) Charly de Salnicks and (Best of Breed) Zula de Ubrique.

At the National Specialty Show for Spanish Breeds organized by the Spanish Kennel Club on November 11, 2001, in which all 18 Spanish breeds were represented, the Spanish Water Dog had the highest entry with a total of 115, of which 23 were Open Class males and 37 were Open Class females. The breed was judged solely by Antonio González.

Considering how relatively new the Spanish Water Dog is in Spain, its future looks quite promising, as the breed's registration statistics (according to the RSCE's stud book) have doubled in five years' time. Compared to the other Spanish breeds, the Spanish Water Dog is the leading breed in number of registrations, with 838 in the year 2000 alone, and a total of 4,227 in the period between 1995 and 2000. The breed has more than

SWIMMING COUSINS

The Spanish Water Dog is frequently compared to its Portuguese cousin, the Caõ de Agua, as the Portuguese Water Dog is called in its homeland. The Portuguese dog is larger than the Spanish breed, standing as tall as 23 inches (58.5 cm) and weighing as much as 60 pounds (27 kg) for a full-grown male. The Portuguese Water Dog is heavier boned and possesses a different type of head and a tufted tail, which is carried over the back. Like the Spanish Water Dog, the Portuguese Water Dog has a coat that does not shed, though it is groomed more in the style of the Poodle, in what is usually called the "lion clip."

The two breeds are different when it comes to work ethic, as the Spanish breed tends to work all day without fail, proving to be more focused and reliable in the field. Both breeds are intelligent and trainable, full of energy and industry.

Portuguese Water Dog.

doubled the number of registrations of longer established indigenous breeds such as the Gos d'Atura Catalá (Catalan Shepherd Dog), Galgo Español and Mastín Español (Spanish Mastiff), and also has outnumbered the Dogo Canario, which previously had been the leading Spanish breed.

A LOOK AT THE BREED'S BEGINNINGS

Thus far, we have studied the more recent history of the Spanish Water Dog and seen how the efforts of a few enthusiastic people allowed this new breed to reach a favored position inside and outside Spain, in a short period of just 15 years. Yet little is known for certain about the breed's origins, thus hypothesis and speculation have given way to legends.

Although a gifted water retriever, as its name indicates, the breed is perhaps more well known in its homeland as a talented and tireless herding dog.

CURLY DOGS
The Spanish Water Dog has certain morphological characteristics that make the non-expert eye mistake it for other breeds such as the Portuguese Water Dog, the Poodle, the Hungarian Puli, the Italian Lagota or the French Barbet. However, there are many traits that distinguish the Spanish breed from the rest.

First of all, shepherding has always been a traditional practice in Spain. In order for this activity to be successful and allow people to make a living—given the varied weather conditions in the Iberian Peninsula—annual migrations were implemented from summer to winter pasturelands and vice-versa. This practice in search of "greener pastures" is known as a seasonal migration (the Spanish word for this is *trashumancia*).

Driving large herds of cattle from one place to another was not easy in and of itself, and the threat of wolves and other wild beasts complicated matters further. For this reason, dogs were assigned an increasingly significant role in the shepherding society, as dogs were useful firstly for hunting and secondly for herding sheep and cattle. The hunting function, of course, came first, and shepherding came later when the larger settlements were established.

The evolution of different kinds of dogs was propelled by the environment in which each dog was needed to work as well as by the task that the dog was expected to perform. The more specific the task and the more demanding the situation, the more specialized was the dog that developed. The large, powerful, fearless mastiffs were called upon for protection and brute strength (pulling heavy loads, warring, etc.). The smaller, more agile dogs developed and became indispensable in cattle droving and moving sheep and other livestock.

The dog we know today as the Spanish Water Dog is one of these smaller useful dogs, along with other native Spanish breeds such as the Ca de Bestiar, the Carea from Castilla, the Carea from Lean, the Garofiano of the Isla of Palma, the Gos d'Atura Catalá and the Majorero. Some of these indigenous breeds already have been recognized officially by the Spanish Kennel Club and/or the FCI, while others are still in the process of being accepted. These unique breeds are tangible evidence of the great variety of shepherd dogs that exists in Spain today, all of which possess specific breed type, physical and mental traits that correspond perfectly to the environments in which they work.

The Spanish Water Dog, which had been known previously as the Turkish Andalusian, seems to have originated from the same family tree as the Barbet of France. The name "Barbet" comes from the French *barbe* (meaning "long beard"), which can be traced further back to the ancient *Canis aquaticus* or water dog. This water dog hunts birds and is very difficult to find nowadays, some 21.5–23.5 inches (55–60 cm) high with a shiny, thick coat in locks of black, gray and solid-colored brown hair, with white markings. This dog is considered to be the "father" of all Spanish Water Dogs as well as the basis of the other water-dog breeds (such as the Portuguese Water Dog and the Irish Water Spaniel).

Maybe the Spanish Water

GENUS *CANIS*

Dogs and wolves are members of the genus *Canis*. Wolves are known scientifically as *Canis lupus* while dogs are known as *Canis domesticus*. Dogs and wolves are known to interbreed. The term *canine* derives from the Latin-derived word *canis*. The term *dog* has no scientific basis but has been used for thousands of years. The origin of the word *dog* has never been authoritatively ascertained.

The American Water Spaniel is counted among the world's water dogs. This breed evolved in the US, where it is used mainly as a hunting dog in the Midwest.

The Barbet of France is believed to be one of the Poodle's ancestors, as well as a cousin of the Spanish Water Dog.

Dog's ancestors—the Turkish Andalusians—were the original "Spanish water dogs" mentioned in 10th-century writings. Their traits were described in those years with accuracy, revealing an undeniable resemblance to the dogs we know today, especially regarding coat, temperament and behavior. Other hypotheses sustain that these dogs could have been introduced into the region of Andalusia by Turkish ships (explaining the use of the old "Turkish Andalusian" name). These dogs worked in the exportation of our Merino sheep to Australia at the end of the 18th and beginning of the 19th centuries. This theory is quite

The Lagotta Romagnolo is Italy's answer to the water dog, though the breed is even more rare than the Spanish Water Dog.

A close cousin, the Portuguese Water Dog is larger than the Spanish Water Dog with a strong following in the US and beyond.

The Puli of Hungary possesses a heavily corded coat and is recognized around the world. Like the Spanish Water Dog, this is a native herding breed from Europe.

reliable since even today on Turkey's coastline, dogs very similar to the Spanish Water Dog continue driving herds back and forth between the docks to the ships.

The very prestigious German breeder Duhel supported the theory of the Asian origins of the Spanish Water Dog. According to him, dogs of the breed accompanied Alanos, Suevos, Vandals and other Barbarian tribes in their successive invasions of Europe. Other experts think that the Spanish Water Dog descended from those that accompanied

Muslims during their years of domination in the peninsula.

The Count of Buffon, Georges Louis Lecrerc (1707–1788), who was appointed as a member of the French Academy in 1753, was noted for writing the famous book entitled *Histoire Naturelle*, concerning the history and "evolution" of animals (birds and quadrupeds). Without actually formulating a formal theory of evolution (which Charles Darwin did later on), Buffon noted that species change with time and that one turns into the degenerated form of another. He held the theory that cattle-raising in the Peninsula was highly influenced by Arabic traditions of the past. Arabs developed their culture in these lands for more than 800 years, which became apparent later, for example, in the way of shearing and washing the wool and of selecting the lambs for reproduction, which were also called *moruecos*.

This also would explain how these people from Northern Africa influenced the dogs that they used to work and drive the herds. Nevertheless, and most curiously, no remains of water dogs similar to the Turkish Andalusian have been found in Northern Africa, from where invaders came, while plenty are found in Turkey. Opponents of this theory use this argument in their attempts to prove it fallible.

THE ANDALUSIAN BIRTHPLACE

To discover the true origins of the Spanish Water Dog, we must account for the fact that the precious Merino sheep were first introduced into Spain by the Ben Merines, a nomadic tribe that

A COAT OF MANY COLORS

A. Flores, M. V. Mañas and J. V. García researched the coat coloration of the breed in Spain in the early 1980s. The study revealed that 61% of the dogs had single-colored coats (predominantly black, followed by chestnut, cinnamon, white, yellow and red), 30% had bicolored markings, 6% had tricolored markings and less than 2% were spotted.

ruled over the South of the Peninsula after the domination of the Almohadies. This makes us hypothesize that they brought the Carea dogs with them to drive their cattle herds.

Based on the autochthonous dogs of Al-Andalus, it is likely that the Carea dogs were also descended from these local dogs but, like with everything else, we must allow for some speculation in this regard. This speculation speaks of the sheep's grazing in the ancient *Baeticus*—which is the Roman name given to the Spanish region located approximately in the area occupied today by Andalusia—and speaks even further of the importance of the local wool cattle, which presented the possibility of tremendously profitable exports in the Turdetan region (Turdetania, Western Betica, formed by the provinces of Huelva and part of Cordoba, Malaga, Cadiz and Seville). A Carea dog of pure Andalusian origins drove the herds. Concrete proof of the importance that cattle had in the area during this period was found in 1981. Composed of bronze, this magnificently designed object, dating back to the fourth or fifth centuries BC, was discovered near Cordoba. It was baptized the "Lamb of Villa-franquina."

Regardless of the specific birthplace of the Spanish Water Dog, the breed traditionally has been associated with a variety of areas. Even if the so-called "Turkish dogs" were found in Almeria, Cadiz, Cordoba, Granada, Malaga and Seville, researchers also have found remains in other areas. They were found scattered throughout Huelva, Jaen and Asturias, Cantabria and the Basque country. Maybe other dogs with similar characteristics can also be found in other regions, doing a variety of tasks associated with the breed, including herding, hunting, guarding and aquatic activities.

THE SPANISH WATER DOG BEYOND ITS NATIONAL BOUNDARIES

THE BREED IN THE UNITED STATES
The first Spanish Water Dogs to enter the US did so in 1997 and were greeted by an enthusiastic, ever-growing fancy. The breed is developing slowly but steadily, aided by its parent club, the Spanish Water Dog Association of America (SWDAA), which was established in 2001. There are about 100 Spanish Water Dogs in the US. The American Kennel Club presently does not recognize the breed, though dogs can be shown at events held by the American Rare Breed Association (ARBA), the National Kennel Club (NKC) and the United Kennel Club (UKC). The SWDAA holds an annual specialty that attracts many excellent dogs from both coasts.

THE WOOLLY BREED GOES TO ENGLAND
The author is grateful to Faye Allen, one of the first breeders to import the dogs to the UK, for the following information about the

SKIN COLOR
The skin of the Spanish Water Dog can be pigmented in black or chestnut, or, on the contrary, it can be completely non-pigmented with a light pink tone.

If your local laws allow, you and your Spanish Water Dogs will enjoy nothing as much as visiting the parks and lakes in your hometown. Spanish Water Dog owners must live within driving distance of at least one body of water (or own a swimming pool!).

breed's entry into Great Britain:
Little did four people from England realize what they were letting themselves in for when they visited Valencia for the World Dog Show in June 1992. Two of them watched a woolly breed in the show ring and then two others saw a demonstration in the main arena. Independently they talked about the two instances, not realizing at first that they were discussing the same breed. It was only when they visited the Spanish breed stands that they found out that they were interested in the same breed of dog—the Perro de Agua Español.

Cutting a long story short, the Canagua Partnership was formed,

with Audrey Murray from Lincolnshire and Christine McQueeney, Diane Philipson and Faye Allen from Manchester. Two Spanish Water Dogs were imported in October 1992: Spanish Ch. Cila de Ubrique (a white bitch) and Topo de Ubrique (a cream dog). These were followed soon after by two more, imported in January 1993, both black and white—Relampago de Ubrique (a dog) and Dilita de Ubrique (a bitch). All four imports came through the necessary quarantine well and, when released, it was as though they had only just arrived. The British breeders were pleased that the imported dogs all possessed the

While bitches mature much earlier than males, usually when they are just six or seven months old, males grow larger than females by about 2 inches.

The soulful, quizzical stare of the Spanish Water Dog has endeared the breed to many sensitive dog lovers.

lovely breed temperament that had impressed them so much when they had visited Spain.

The Canagua Partnership's first litter was born on October 9, 1993. From a mating of Relampago de Ubrique to Dilita de Ubrique, there were three puppies: Canagua el Mejor, a brown and white dog; Canagua Llamativo Senora, a white and black bitch; and Canagua Pescador Amigo, a cream dog.

The Kennel Club accepted the breed in October 1992, although dogs could not be shown until 2001, when the dogs were eligible for the Import Register Classes. The breed is not currently eligible for Challenge Certificates, which are necessary to gain a championship in the UK. The Spanish Water Dog Club of England works to maintain the best qualities of these dogs before popularity rears its ugly head and spoils them. Likewise, the members of the Canagua Partnership consider themselves as the guardians of the breed in Britain and wish to keep the Spanish Water Dogs true to their native country. The British fanciers encourage the natural working ability of these exceptional dogs. Since the early 1990s, the Canagua Spanish Water Dogs have taken part in many gundog, water, agility and flyball events and competitions with successful results.

Spanish Ch.
Bartolo
represents
everything
lovable and
admirable in the
breed, including
an irresistible
smile.

CHARACTERISTICS OF THE
SPANISH WATER DOG

According to legend, Napoleon fell in love with the ancestors of the Spanish Water Dog and brought a few dogs back to France with him. The emperor was fascinated by the dog's ability to drove cattle in the field or to dive into the water to depths of 10 feet or more. It's of course possible that the Spanish dogs that Napoleon imported could be somehow related to the French water dogs of today.

The appeal of the Spanish Water Dog quite obviously is accorded to the breed's tremendous working capacity—on land and water—as well as his vivacious temperament, his beguiling appearance and his superior intelligence. Whether you are making the acquaintance of this friendly, personable dog as a companion dog or as a skilled hunter and worker, you are meeting a truly extraordinary wonder of the dog world.

EXCEPTIONAL ADAPTABILITY
This is an exceptionally adaptable dog, capable of working in various environments, from muddy swamps to arid desert-like plains. As skilled in the pasture as a trained Border Collie, the Spanish Water Dog can change gears and swim out after ducks or dive underwater to catch fish that escape the fisherman's net. The Perro de Agua Español can do anything you ask him to do—and probably on the same day! For the breed's many and varied skills, it is gaining new fanciers around the world—and surely the appealing photographs in this book will win this brilliant little dog even more devoted followers.

UTILITY, INTELLIGENCE AND TEMPERAMENT
Such an adaptable dog has indeed to be very useful. With tremendous hardiness and resistance to disease, the Spanish Water Dog adjusts to the environment, no

ACTIVE MINDS
Faye Allen shares with us, "This breed can turn its paws to anything. They have terrific memories and are extremely quick learners, but bright dogs are quick to learn bad habits as well as good. Judging by the behavior of all the youngsters seen, they need something to do as their brains need working."

matter how harsh conditions can be. He is at home in both cold and warm places, as long as he's given a task to accomplish and a master to love and serve. Despite the breed's many uses, these dogs are mainly used today for herding, which they have been doing for many hundreds of years. Their list of duties, however, continues to expand, and the Spanish Water Dog is also employed for guarding, hunting, fishing and other aquatic activities, as well as for companionship.

As a shepherd dog, the Spanish Water Dog is capable of driving large herds of cattle with amazing efficiency. The dog does not need any training to do this work; his instinctive knowledge of the task shows very strongly from puppyhood. Thus, the shepherd only needs to choose the pup who is animated around cattle to single out the dog who will excel as a herder.

The shepherd only needs to lead the Perro de Agua Español by signaling with his hands or by using certain voice commands. More often than not, the intuitive and lively Spanish Water Dog takes initiative and performs with little instruction. This is one of the breed's most distinctive characteristics, one that it shares with its fellow native herder, the Gos d'Atura Catalá. In fact, the dogs are always vigilant at work, knowing when to herd the cattle and control it from going out of the designated borders.

It is interesting to note that Spanish Water Dogs perform their herding tasks while running quickly and with amazing agility, leaping and turning almost like acrobats, barking if necessary and rarely biting. That is why the Spanish shepherds rarely muzzle their dogs or cut their canine teeth, which is often done to other breeds. Only as a last resort will the Spanish Water Dog bite its most recalcitrant charges, and then only in the hock or leg.

The Spanish Water Dog also is capable of moving in the water as easily as he does on *terra firma*. Actually, the breed was used in the past on the borders of the Guadalquivir River in Seville to help ships reach the docks. The dogs' job was to catch the ships' ropes with their mouths and pull them to the docks or land. Even today, although not often, these dogs are still used in aquatic activities along the northern coastline of Spain. They are specially used as fishing dogs in regions of Asturias, Cantabria and the Basque country, where they dive to retrieve the fish that escape from the nets. These dogs actually have developed such swimming skills that their legs have adjusted perfectly to the exercise and their specially structured feet work as oars, allowing them to move forward easily in the water.

In recent years, many breed fanciers have learned to appreciate the Spanish Water Dog's capacity and instincts for hunting, and have begun to use these dogs more frequently in rabbit hunting or for retrieving duck in rivers and swamps. The breed's agile and buoyant body structure, sensitive nose and thick coat allows it to enter thick forests or the coldest waters with a bold and fearless fervor. The dogs do not suffer from colds or other ailments that might be associated with such extreme temperatures.

The Spanish Water Dog does not trust strangers, which makes him an excellent watchdog. Many fanciers also have begun to train the breed in advanced obedience. Since the dog learns so fast, he immediately responds to commands and works as a guardian with energy and eagerness.

Their playful, gay temperament makes them especially attractive as companion dogs, although it is necessary to provide the dogs with ample outdoor exercise opportunities. If allowed to become sedentary and lazy, the dogs will lose their charm and inspiration. Keep Spanish Water Dogs active and they will be happy and rewarding companions.

The Spanish Water Dog achieves a special understanding with his human family and is especially tolerant with children. He treats young family members

DIVING DIVAS
There are Spanish Water Dogs capable of diving 3 to 4 yards underwater without difficulty!

as he does his charges in the field, with equal consideration and intelligent handling. It is curious to see one of these dogs in the grass, trying to keep five or six children together as if they were straying sheep! The dogs do it with the same seriousness and devotion—leaping, turning, pivoting in the air, barking gaily—but they do not bite, not even accidentally as do some other herding breeds.

Nevertheless, the Spanish Water Dog, just like most other working dogs, usually prefers one single member of the family, whom he understands to be his master or "boss." The dog will take orders more consistently from his boss than from anyone else. That is why it is important to teach dogs from puppyhood to take obedience orders from all family members in any given circumstance or at any time. In this way, if the boss is not present for whatever reason, the animal will not fail to obey. Likewise, all members of the family should offer the dog's food to him so that he does not accept his food only from his "boss."

MALES VS. FEMALES

As it happens in most breeds, and in the case of the Spanish Water Dog, females grow mature before males do, usually when they are six or seven months old. It is at this time that bitches first experience their heat cycles. Males, on the contrary, stay playful like puppies until they are approximately one year old. This explains how bitches seem to be more capable of working in the fields earlier in life than males. This does not mean that males are not capable of doing so, they just require more instruction and patience.

In general, bitches are slightly smaller in height at the withers (an average of 1.5–2 in or 3–5 cm less than males) and also lighter in weight (approximately 6–9 lb or 3–4 kg less). However, size usually is not a deciding factor when choosing a medium-sized dog like the Spanish Water Dog. There is also a slight difference regarding head dimensions. Males usually have broader, more elongated heads than females, but heads should always be in proportion to the size and weight of the animal.

BREED-SPECIFIC HEALTH CONCERNS

While the Spanish Water Dog is indeed an ancient dog, it is still an infant in terms of its modern history. Breeders have not had the benefit of many generations of research to warn new and potential owners about the hereditary diseases that affect the breed. Although there have been only a few such incidences, the Spanish Water Dog is likely prone to hip dysplasia as well as to any of a number of eye conditions, such as progressive retinal atrophy (PRA), collie eye anomaly and cataracts.

The breed shares a similar lineage and body type with the Portuguese Water Dog, a breed on which there is significant genetic research regarding cardiomyopathy, follicular dysplasia,

Before purchasing your Spanish Water Dog puppy, be certain the breeder has screened his stock for known hereditary problems.

storage disease, Addison's disease, distichiasis, gangliodidisosis, hypoadrenocorticism, hypothyroidism and microophthalmia. It is wise to share this information with your vet as he likely does not have experience with the Spanish Water Dog (or Portuguese Water Dog). Let us look at some of these conditions more closely.

PROGRESSIVE RETINAL ATROPHY (PRA)

PRA is a condition in which retinal cells degenerate, eventually causing blindness. It is a genetic disease that affects many purebred dogs. Breeders expect that late-onset PRA is more likely to affect the breed, beginning in dogs three to five years of age. For this disease and other eye diseases, dogs should be registered with the Canine Eye Registration Foundation (CERF) and all dogs should be evaluated annually by a qualified ophthalmologist. Be certain that the sire and dam of your puppy is CERF-registered.

CATARACTS

Characterized by a lens opacity that affects one or both eyes, cataracts may involve a portion of the entire lens. Hardly noticeable to the naked eye, a cataract usually develops as a small white area and can result from various things, such as trauma, inflammation and nutritional deficiencies, as well as from diabetes.

DOGS, DOGS, GOOD FOR YOUR HEART!

People usually purchase dogs for companionship, but studies show that dogs can help to improve their owners' health and level of activity, as well as lower a human's risk of coronary heart disease. Without even realizing it, when a person puts time into exercising, grooming and feeding a dog, he also puts more time into his own personal health care. Dog owners establish more routine schedules for their dogs to follow, which can have positive effects on their own health. Dogs also teach us patience, offer unconditional love and provide the joy of having a woolly friend to pet!

DISTICHIASIS

A dog affected by distichiasis may suffer from eye irritation caused by improperly located eyelashes. Likely hereditary, the disease can appear in dogs of any age.

STORAGE DISEASE

A condition produced by a recessive gene, storage disease only affects dogs that obtain a defective gene from two affected parents. The disease is characterized by the lack of certain types of enzyme, thus allowing a build-up of toxic substances in the nerve cells.

ADDISON'S DISEASE

Caused by an adrenocortical hormone deficiency, Addison's disease affects middle-aged dogs. Symptoms include lethargy, vomiting, diarrhea, inappetence and other rather generic signs of ill health. Your vet should test your dog for this condition if these signs persist. If diagnosed early enough, the disease can be treated through hormone-replacement therapy.

FOLLICULAR DYSPLASIA

This hair-loss disorder usually affects curly-coated dogs. Hair loss occurs mainly on the chest, flanks, back, abdomen and around the anus, and possibly around one or both eyes. There is no effective therapy at present.

DO YOU KNOW ABOUT HIP DYSPLASIA?

Hip dysplasia is a condition sometimes found in Spanish Water Dogs, as well as in other breeds. When a dog has hip dysplasia, his hind leg has an incorrectly formed hip joint. By constant use of the hip joint, it becomes more and more loose, wears abnormally and may become arthritic.

Hip dysplasia can only be confirmed with an x-ray, but certain symptoms may indicate a problem. Your Spanish Water Dog may have a hip dysplasia problem if he walks in a peculiar manner, hops instead of smoothly running, uses his hinds legs in unison (to keep the pressure off the weak joint), has trouble getting up from a prone position and always sits with both legs together on one side of his body. As the dog matures, he may adapt well to life with a bad hip, but in a few years the arthritis develops and many dogs with hip dysplasia become crippled. Hip dysplasia is considered an inherited disease and can be definitively diagnosed when the dog is two years old.

Some experts claim that a special diet might help your puppy outgrow the bad hip, but the usual treatments are surgical. The removal of the pectineus muscle, the removal of the round part of the femur, reconstructing the pelvis and replacing the hip with an artificial one are some treatment options. All of these surgical interventions are expensive, but they are usually very successful. Follow the advice of your veterinarian.

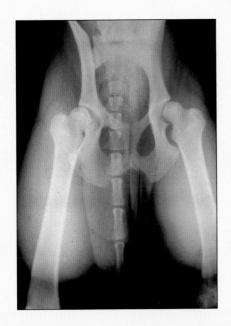

Compare the two hip joints and you'll understand dysplasia better. Hip dysplasia is a badly worn hip joint caused by improper fit of the bone into the socket. It is easily the most common hip problem in dogs.
Left: X-ray of "moderate" dysplastic hips.
Below left: X-ray of "good" hips.

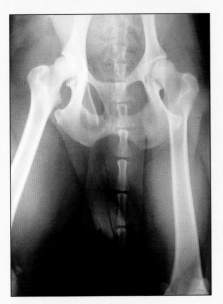

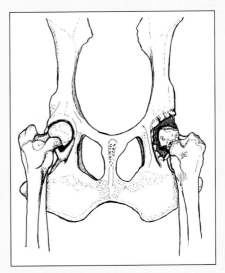

The healthy hip joint on the left and the unhealthy hip joint on the right.

BREED STANDARD FOR THE

SPANISH WATER DOG

A breed standard is a written description of the ideal representative of a breed. This description is used by judges, breeders and exhibitors to guide them in their selection, breeding and promotion of the best dogs. At dog shows, the judges compare each dog entered to the dog described in each breed's respective standard. The dog that most closely "conforms" to its breed standard is selected as the winner. For this reason, dog shows are sometimes called "conformation competitions."

Breed standards in America are drafted by the parent club (the Spanish Water Dog Association of America) and then approved by the national kennel club (AKC, UKC, NKC or ARBA);

Whether you are seeking a pet- or show-quality Spanish Water Dog, you must not compromise on the soundness and type of the dog. This handsome dog is eight years old and still looking dapper.

A dog showing correct balance, type and structure, with mature, natural curly coat.

in England, the breed standard is devised by The Kennel Club, with some input by key breeders and judges. Although standards vary from country to country, and kennel club to kennel club, they are essentially the same with minor differences in word choice, emphasis and detail. Here we present an English translation of the Spanish standard, which is the standard recognized by the Spanish Royal Canine Society and the FCI.

THE FCI STANDARD FOR THE SPANISH WATER DOG

ORIGIN
Spain.

UTILIZATION
Used as shepherd dog, hunting dog and assistant to the fisherman.

CLASSIFICATION
Group 8 Retrievers/Flushing Dogs, Section 3 Water Dogs, without working trial.

HEAD STUDIES SHOWING CORRECT TYPE AND STRUCTURE

Clipped coat, grown out enough to show characteristic curl.

Natural untrimmed appearance.

BRIEF HISTORICAL SUMMARY

The presence of this dog in the Iberian Peninsula is most ancient. His origin is the same as that of the old Barbet. His most dense population is in Andalusia where he is used as a shepherd dog, and where he has been known for centuries as the Turkish dog. His characteristics, most particularly the quality of his coat, are adapted to the variation of humidity and drought of the marshy regions, which qualifies him as a shepherd dog and as a helper to the hunters of waterfowl and fishermen in those regions.

GENERAL APPEARANCE

Rustic dog, well proportioned (medium weight), dolicho-cephalic, of rather elongated harmonious shape and attractive appearance, of an athletic nature with well-developed muscles owing to his regular exercise; the profile is rectilinear; his sight, hearing and scent are well developed.

IMPORTANT PROPORTIONS

- Length of body/size (height at withers) = 9/8.
- Depth of chest/size (height at withers) = 4/8.
- Length of muzzle/length of skull = 2/3.

BEHAVIOR/TEMPERAMENT

Faithful, obedient, gay, hard working, watchful and well balanced. Learning ability is outstanding owing to his extraordinary mental grasp; he adapts to all situations and conditions.

HEAD

Strong, carried with elegance.

CRANIAL REGION

Skull: Flat with only slightly marked occipital crest. Direction of axes of skull and muzzle parallel. *Stop:* Facial-cranial depression slightly marked.

FACIAL REGION

Profile is rectilinear. *Nose:* Nostrils well defined. Nose is of the same color or slightly darker than the darkest one of the coat. *Lips:* Well fitting; labial corners well defined. *Teeth:* Well-formed, white, with well-developed canines. *Eyes:* Slightly oblique position, very expressive; of a hazel to chestnut color, should harmonize with the color of the coat. The conjunctiva is not apparent. *Ears:* Set at medium height, triangular drooping.

NECK

Short, well muscled, without dewlap, springing cleanly into the shoulders.

BODY

Robust. *Topline:* Straight. *Withers:* Hardly marked. *Back:* Straight and powerful. *Chest:* Broad and well let down; ribs well arched: diameter of thorax ample, indicating considerable respiratory capacity. *Rump (croup):* Slightly tucked up.

TAIL

Set at medium height. Docking must be done at the height of the second to the fourth vertebra. Certain subjects show a congenital shortened tail (brachyury).

LIMBS

Forequarters: Strong and vertical. *Shoulders:* Well muscled and oblique. *Upper arms:* Sturdy. *Elbows:* Close to the chest and parallel. *Forearms:* Straight and sturdy. *Carpus (Pastern joint) and pastern:* Straight, rather short. *Front feet:* Rounded, toes tight, nails of varied colors, strong resistant pads.

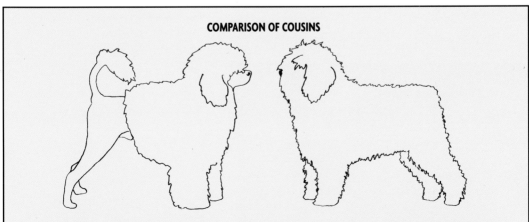

COMPARISON OF COUSINS

Portuguese Water Dog (left) is a bit taller and square in appearance with a longer neck. This dog is shown in a lion clip and a wavy coat. Spanish Water Dog (right) is rectangular in appearance with a docked tail and a short, strong neck. This dog is untrimmed.

Hindquarters: Perfectly straight with not too pronounced angulation and muscles capable of transmitting to the body an impulsion full of energy when he runs and the spring necessary for easy and elegant jumping. *Upper thighs:* Large and well muscled. *Second thighs:* Well developed. *Hock joint:* Well let down. *Hock:* Short, lean and perpendicular to the ground. *Hind feet:* As the forefeet.

GAIT/MOVEMENT

The preferred gait is the trot. The gallop is short and jerky.

SKIN

Supple, fine and well adhering to the body. Can be pigmented brown or black, or be without pigment according to the color of the coat. The same applies to the mucus membranes.

COAT

Hair: Always curly and of woolly texture. Curly when short, can

By acquiring a well-bred Spanish Water Dog, you will be assured that your dog will be able to run and play for his whole life. Structural problems can render an otherwise healthy dog lame and crippled.

BREEDING CONSIDERATIONS
The decision to breed your dog is one that must be considered carefully and researched thoroughly before moving into action. Some people believe that breeding will make their bitches happier or that it is an easy way to make money. Unfortunately, indiscriminate breeding only worsens the rampant problem of pet overpopulation, as well as being detrimental to the entire breed. As for the bitch, the entire process from mating through whelping is not an easy one and puts your pet under considerable stress. Last, but not least, consider whether or not you have the means to care for an entire litter of pups.

form cords when long. Clipped subjects are admitted; the clipping, always complete and even, must never become (esthetic) grooming. The recommended maximum length of the hair for show is 12 cm (15 cm extending the curl) and the minimum is 3 cm to see the quality of the curl. Puppies always are born with curly hair.

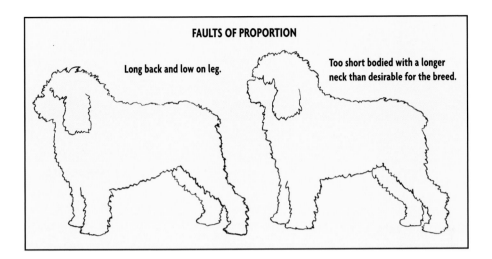

FAULTS OF PROPORTION

Long back and low on leg.

Too short bodied with a longer neck than desirable for the breed.

COLOR

Solid: White, black and chestnut in different shades. *Bicolor:* White and black or white and brown in different shades.
Tricolor, black and tan as well as hazelnut and tan dogs are not admitted.

SIZE

Height at withers: Males 44–50 cm (17.32–19.69 in); females 40–46 cm (15.75–18.11 in). 2 cm (.78 in) maximum deviation are admitted in both sexes whenever the subject maintains balance according to height at withers.
Weight: Males 18–22 kg (39.69–48.5 lb); females 14–18 kg (30.86–39.69 lb).

FAULTS

Any departure from the foregoing points should be considered a fault and the seriousness with which the fault should be regarded should be in exact proportion to its degree.

SERIOUS FAULTS

- Dorso-lumbar region distinctly saddle-backed.
- Limbs incorrect.
- Belly let down or excessively tucked up.

DISQUALIFYING FAULTS

- Inferior or superior prognathism.
- Presence of dewclaws.
- Smooth or wavy coat.
- Albinism.
- Spotty or flecked coat, black and tan or chestnut and tan coat.
- Lack of balance in character.
- Evident timidity or aggressiveness.

N.B.: Male animals should have two apparently normal testicles fully descended into the scrotum.

SPANISH WATER DOG

SELECTING THE PUPPY

Before deciding to purchase a Spanish Water Dog puppy, you must decide how well this active breed will fit into your family and lifestyle. While he is happy and fun to be around, this dog has more energy than most breeds and will need to find outlets to release it. To be fair to the dog and to your family, the Spanish Water Dog must fit in with your established routine or else all concerned, dog and human, will be discontent. Talk to the breeder and other owners who love this breed and find out for yourself what is required for ownership.

The author suggests that you attend a rare-breed dog show where the breed is presented. In the United States, the American Rare Breed Association (ARBA) presents shows all around the country; in England, The Kennel Club offers classes for Imports. If you are fortunate enough to travel to Spain or elsewhere on the Continent, you may be able to attend an FCI show or even a Spanish specialty show. Don't forget to enlist a translator for the field trip.

If there are no dog shows in your area or such a trip is not feasible, at least you will have the chance to speak on the telephone with breeders and owners to find

TEMPERAMENT COUNTS

Your selection of a good puppy can be determined by your needs. A show potential or a good pet? It is your choice. Every puppy, however, should be of good temperament. Although show-quality puppies are bred and raised with emphasis on physical conformation, responsible breeders strive for equally good temperament. Do not buy from a breeder who concentrates solely on physical beauty at the expense of personality.

out as much about the breed as possible. Likewise, if there is a breeder within driving distance, it will be worth the effort to visit his kennel to see the dogs in person. Do not be afraid to ask questions…and then ask some more questions! This is essential, even if you know the answers or the answers seem pretty obvious. Compare the answers provided by each person in the breed whom you meet. This is the best way to get a more complete picture of the Spanish Water Dog.

Despite your enthusiasm— fueled, no doubt, by the many adorable photos in this book— there really is no hurry and it is best not to have an appointed day (like a birthday or any other specific family celebration) to choose a puppy. By and large, you will likely not have the option of rushing into the purchase of a

The Spanish Water Dog is an active, alert breed that requires an owner who is on her toes! Are you up for the challenge of such a "get-up-and-gone" breed?

puppy because the demand for these puppies far outweighs the supply. With a rare-breed puppy, you will have to be content with being placed on a waiting list and hope for a puppy to arrive within a year (or two!).

The last decade has been miraculous for the Spanish Water Dog, but this does not mean that it will much easier to find a quality puppy. You must find a sound, healthy and typical Spanish Water Dog puppy—not the only puppy you can locate on your seaboard! Just as if you were purchasing a more popular breed like the Poodle or Cocker Spaniel, you must always insist on finding a

---

YOUR SCHEDULE . . .

If you lead an erratic, unpredictable life, with daily or weekly changes in your work requirements, consider the problems of owning a puppy. The new puppy has to be fed regularly, socialized (loved, petted, handled, introduced to other people) and, most importantly, allowed to go outdoors for house-training. As the dog gets older, he can be more tolerant of deviations in his feeding and relief schedule.

PUPPY APPEARANCE

Your puppy should have a well-fed appearance but not a distended abdomen, which may indicate worms or incorrect feeding, or both. The body should be firm, with a solid feel. The skin of the abdomen should be pale pink and clean, without signs of scratching or rash. Check to make sure that the breeder has had the dewclaws removed.

going to be timid about treating your rare and delicate cargo.

No one can tell you better about the breed and the puppy than the puppy's breeder. A responsible, conscientious breeder produces only sound dogs and makes demands upon his potential puppy buyers. Such a breeder usually will have a longer waiting list and, therefore, it will take him longer to provide you with a contract. Even with a breed as rare as the Perro de Agua Español, you cannot trust a breeder who is anxious to sell you a puppy, has no time for your questions, only wants to discuss the price and will have a puppy available to you around Christmas! This breeder is not doing you (or his poor puppies) any favors!

Once you have located and chosen a breeder, you are ready to visit the kennels. A well-maintained kennel will be clean and inviting, a place where happy, clean and healthy-looking *perros* live and welcome visitors. Remember that the Spanish Water Dog is not instantly approachable like the Golden Retriever, so the dogs may take some time to warm up to you. However, this does not mean that the dogs will run away, and they should act comfortable around familiar people like the breeder and his family. If you have a doubt about the kennel, it is

properly bred and socialized puppy. A problem puppy is a problem, no matter how rare the breed. Likewise, if you acquire an unhealthy puppy of this breed, your vet may be intimidated. He probably never has met a Spanish Water Dog and, sensibly or not, may be afraid to treat the dog in the same way he would a sick Cocker or Sheltie pup, breeds with which he's had lots of experience. When you select your vet, be sure you find one who is not

ARE YOU PREPARED?

Unfortunately, when a puppy is bought by someone who does not take into consideration the time and attention that dog ownership requires, it is the puppy who suffers when he is either abandoned or placed in a shelter by a frustrated owner. So all of the "homework" you do in preparation for your pup's arrival will benefit you both. The more informed you are, the more you will know what to expect and the better equipped you will be to handle the ups and downs of raising a puppy. Hopefully, everyone in the household is willing to do his part in raising and caring for the pup. The anticipation of owning a dog often brings a lot of promises from excited family members: "I will walk him every day," "I will feed him," "I will house-train him," etc., but these things take time and effort, and promises can easily be forgotten once the novelty of the new pet has worn off.

an important consideration, and neither is gender in this breed (unless you plan to breed or show the dog).

If you really have chosen a good breeder, he will know which dog is best for you, your lifestyle and your expectations. This is one reason that breeders will ask you so many personal questions. A responsible breeder deserves your trust and your complete cooperation. Such a breeder takes notes and will likely ask you to fill out a questionnaire about your personality, living conditions, etc. The breeder wants to guarantee that you get the right dog and that his puppy has the right home in which to thrive and be happy for the rest of his days.

The best age at which to

always better to proceed with caution instead of committing to a puppy that does not satisfy your expectations.

When selecting a puppy from a litter, leave your color and gender preconceptions home! All Spanish Water Dogs are attractive, regardless of color. Do not decide that you will only purchase a red and white female puppy or a solid brown male puppy. Color is not

A quintessential family dog, the Spanish Water Dog savors the companionship of the entire family. The whole family should be involved in the care of its canine member.

choose a Spanish Water Dog puppy is eight weeks. You must recognize what a healthy, typical puppy looks like at this age. Let's look at some of the desirable characteristics at this age:

- The puppy looks like an adult in miniature—a "photocopy" reduced in size;
- He will be a happy and furious little tyke who wants to win over his visitor's attention, not continuing to shy away from you (which is OK at first, given the reserved nature of this breed);
- He will be thin but showing some growing muscles, mostly on the legs. The belly should not appear bloated or swollen (unless the pup has just finished eating). A pot-belly can indicate possible parasite infestation;
- Feet will be rounded and tight, with short nails and moist foot pads; the nose also will be moist;
- The eyes will be clean, not teary, but moist and shiny, not showing the conjunctiva;
- The inside of the ears will be clean, pink and shiny;
- The coat will be clean and shiny, free of parasites; there will no missing hair patches on the elbows or hocks. The puppy will basically be free of doggy odor, except the characteristic "baby" smell;
- There will be no fecal matter around the anus nor discharge from the genitals;
- The puppy's gait or movement will be loose but show determination, rather agile for his young age in spite of the clumsiness that characterizes puppies of any breed at this age. His legs will not cross when he runs and he will approach when he is called and accept the visitor's petting;
- Even at this age, the puppy should begin to represent the standard, when viewed from the front or rear;
- The male pup will already look a little bit more masculine than the female, and both genders already will have all of the characteristics of the breed;
- The puppy's bite should not appear undershot nor overshot at this age. Puppy bites rarely improve and usually only worsen in adulthood;
- Whether solid or bicolor, the color will be clear without spotting (and never tricolored).

When you select your puppy, you are well advised to meet the dam of the litter, too. How she reacts with her brood will indicate much about the future personality of your chosen pup.

PREPARING PUPPY'S PLACE IN YOUR HOME

Researching your breed and finding a breeder are only two aspects of the homework you will have to do before collecting your Spanish Water Dog puppy. You will also have to prepare your home and family for the new addition. Much as you would prepare a nursery for a newborn baby, you will need to designate a place in your home that will be the puppy's own. How you prepare your home will depend on how much freedom the dog will be allowed. Whatever you decide, you must ensure that he has a place that he can "call his own."

When you bring your new puppy into your home, you are bringing him into what will become his home as well. Obviously, you did not buy a puppy with the intentions of catering to his every whim and allowing him to "rule the roost,"

These tiny water babies still have a few weeks to go before they can receive visitors, and a few weeks after that before they will be ready to leave the breeder to go to their new homes.

but in order for a puppy to grow into a stable, well-adjusted dog, he has to feel comfortable in his surroundings. Remember, he is leaving the warmth and security of his mother and littermates, as well as the familiarity of the only place he has ever known, so it is important to make his transition as easy as possible.

By preparing a place in your home for the puppy, you are making him feel as welcome as possible in a strange new place. It should not take him long to get used to it, but the sudden shock of being transplanted is somewhat traumatic for a young pup. Imagine how a small child would feel in the same situation—that is how your puppy must be feeling. It is up to you to reassure him and to let him know, "Little *perro*, you are going to like it here!"

WHAT YOU SHOULD BUY

CRATE

To someone unfamiliar with the use of crates in dog training, it may seem like punishment to shut

TIME TO GO HOME

Breeders rarely release puppies until they are eight to ten weeks of age. This is an acceptable age for most breeds of dog, excepting toy breeds, which are not released until around 12 weeks, given their petite sizes. If a breeder has a puppy that is 12 weeks of age or older, he is likely well socialized and house-trained. Be sure that he is otherwise healthy before deciding to take him home.

Your local pet shop should have a wide selection of dog crates from which you can choose the most suitable crate for your Spanish Water Dog.

PHOTO COURTESY OF DOSKOCIL.

training. For example, crate training is a popular and successful house-training method. In addition, a crate can keep your dog safe during travel and, perhaps most importantly, a crate provides your dog with a place of his own in your home. It serves as a "doggie bedroom" of sorts—your Spanish Water Dog puppy can curl up in his crate when he wants to sleep or when he just needs a break. Many dogs sleep in their crates overnight. With soft bedding and his favorite toy, a crate becomes a cozy pseudo-den for your dog. Like his ancestors, he too will seek out the comfort and retreat of a den— you just happen to be providing him with something a little more luxurious than what his early ancestors enjoyed.

As far as purchasing a crate, the type that you buy is up to you. It will most likely be one of the two most popular types: wire or fiberglass. There are advantages and disadvantages to each type. For example, a wire crate is more open, allowing the air to flow through and affording the dog a view of what is going on around him, while a fiberglass crate is sturdier. Both can double as car travel crates, providing protection for the dog.

The size of the crate is another thing to consider. Puppies do not stay puppies forever—in fact, sometimes it seems as if they grow right before your eyes. A

a dog in a crate, but this is not the case at all. Most breeders today recommend crate training, especially in America; breeders in Europe are becoming more supportive of the concept as well. Thus, more and more breeders and trainers are recommending crates as preferred tools for show puppies as well as pet puppies.

Crates are not cruel—crates have many humane and highly effective uses in dog care and

CRATE-TRAINING TIPS

During crate training, you should partition off the section of the crate in which the pup stays. If he is given too big an area, this will hinder your training efforts. Crate training is based on the fact that a dog does not like to soil his sleeping quarters, so it is ineffective to keep a pup in an area that is so big that he can eliminate in one end and get far enough away from it to sleep. Also, you want to make the crate den-like for the pup. Blankets and a favorite toy will make the crate cozy for the small pup; as he grows, you may want to evict some of his "roommates" to make more room. It will take some coaxing at first, but be patient. Given some time to get used to it, your pup will adapt to his new home-within-a-home quite nicely.

small crate may be fine for an eight-week-old Spanish Water Dog pup, but it will not do him much good for long! It's best to purchase a crate that will accommodate your dog both as a puppy and at full size. A large-size crate is best for a full-grown Spanish Water Dog, as it will allow the dog adequate room to sit, stand and lie down comfortably.

BEDDING
A nice plush crate mat will help the dog feel more at home, and you may also like to give him a small blanket. First, these will take the place of the leaves, twigs, etc., that the pup would use in the wild to make a den; the pup can make his own "burrow" in the crate. Although your pup is far removed from his den-making ancestors, the denning instinct is still a part of his genetic make-up. Second, until you take your pup home, he has been sleeping amid the warmth of his mother and littermates, and while a blanket is not the same as a warm, breathing body, it still provides heat and something with which to snuggle. You will want to wash your pup's bedding frequently in case he has a house-training mishap in his crate, and replace or remove any blanket or padding that becomes ragged and starts to fall apart.

TOYS
Toys are a must for dogs of all ages, especially for curious playful pups. Puppies are the "kids" of the dog world, and what child does not love toys? Chew toys

Breeders commonly use "ex-pens" to house their pups during their early training. Such control devices helps to make crate training easier when the time arrives.

TOYS, TOYS, TOYS!

With a big variety of dog toys available, and so many that look like they would be a lot of fun for a dog, be careful in your selection. It is amazing what a set of puppy teeth can do to an innocent-looking toy; so, obviously, safety is a major consideration. Be sure to choose the most durable products that you can find. Hard nylon bones and toys are a safe bet, and many of them are offered in different scents and flavors that will be sure to capture your dog's attention. It is always fun to play a game of fetch with your dog, and there are balls and flying discs that are specially made to withstand dog teeth.

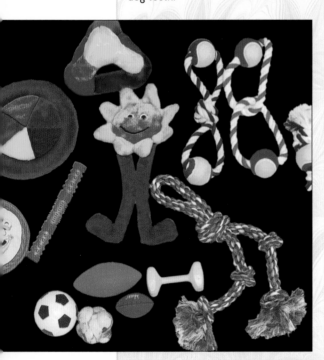

provide enjoyment for both dog and owner—your dog will enjoy playing with his favorite toys, while you will enjoy the fact that they distract him from chewing on your expensive shoes and leather sofa. Puppies love to chew; in fact, chewing is a physical need for pups as they are teething, and everything looks appetizing! The full range of your possessions—from cotton slipper to Oriental carpet—are fair game in the eyes of a teething pup. Puppies are not all that discerning when it comes to finding something literally to "sink their teeth into"—everything tastes great!

Though not an inveterate chewer, a bored Spanish Water Dog with nothing to do and insufficient human contact can become a destructive Spanish Water Dog. Chewing is one way for a dog to release some of the frustration that builds up. To prevent that from occurring, select durable toys of the appropriate size for both puppies and adults and make sure that your dog is receiving the attention he deserves.

Provide your dog with hard, indestructible toys that will last him many months of good chewing. Squeaky and stuffed toys are quite popular, but must be avoided for the Spanish Water Dog. Perhaps one of these can be used as an aid in training, but not for free play. If a pup "disembowels" one of these, the small plastic

FINANCIAL RESPONSIBILITY

Grooming tools, collars, leashes, a crate, a dog bed and, of course, toys will be expenses to you when you first obtain your pup, and the cost will continue throughout your dog's lifetime. If your puppy damages or destroys your possessions (as most puppies surely will!) or something belonging to a neighbor, you can calculate additional expense. There is also flea and pest control, which every dog owner faces more than once. You must be able to handle the financial responsibility of owning a dog.

his leash, he has a very slim chance of being able to chew through the strong nylon. Nylon leashes are also lightweight, which is good for a young Spanish Water Dog who is just getting used to the idea of walking on a leash. For everyday walking and safety purposes, the nylon leash is a good choice.

As your pup grows up and gets used to walking on the leash, you may want to purchase a flexible leash. These leashes allow you to extend the length to give the dog a broader area to explore or to shorten the length to keep the dog near you. Of course, there are leashes designed for training and showing purposes, but these are not necessary or suitable for routine walks.

squeaker or stuffing inside can be dangerous if swallowed. Monitor the condition of all your pup's toys carefully and get rid of any that have been chewed to the point of becoming potentially dangerous.

Be careful of natural bones, which have a tendency to splinter into sharp, dangerous pieces. Also be careful of rawhide, which can turn into pieces that are easy to swallow and become a mushy mess on your carpet.

LEASH

A nylon leash is probably the best option, as it is the most resistant to puppy teeth should your pup take a liking to chewing on his leash. Of course, this is a habit that should be nipped in the bud, but, if your pup likes to chew on

Spanish Water Dog pups are natural athletes, excelling in football and other outdoor sports.

COLLAR

Your pup should get used to wearing a collar all the time since you will want to attach his identification tags to it; plus, you have to attach the leash to something! A lightweight nylon collar is a good choice. Make certain that the collar fits snugly enough so that the pup cannot wriggle out of it, but is loose enough so that it will not be uncomfortably tight around the pup's neck. You should be able to fit a finger between the pup's neck and the collar. It may take some time for your pup to get used to wearing the collar, but soon he will not even notice that it is there. Chain choke collars are made for training, but are not suitable for use on the Spanish Water Dog, as this collar will pull at and possibly damage the breed's abundant woolly coat.

FOOD AND WATER BOWLS

Your pup will need two bowls, one for food and one for water. You may want two sets of bowls, one for indoors and one for outdoors, depending on where the dog will be fed and where he will be spending time. Purchase the largest size you can find. Stainless steel or sturdy plastic bowls are popular choices. Plastic bowls are more chewable, but dogs tend not to chew on the steel variety, which can be sterilized. It is important to buy sturdy bowls since anything is in danger of being chewed by puppy teeth and you do not want your dog to be constantly chewing apart his bowl (for his safety and for your financial stability!).

CLEANING SUPPLIES

Until a pup is house-trained, you will be doing a lot of cleaning. "Accidents" will occur, which is acceptable in the beginning stages of toilet training because the puppy does not know any better. All you can do is be prepared to clean up any accidents as soon as they happen. Old rags, towels, newspapers and a safe disinfectant are good to have on hand.

BEYOND THE BASICS

The items previously discussed are the bare necessities. You will find out what else you need as you go along—grooming supplies, flea/tick protection, baby gates to

CHOOSE AN APPROPRIATE COLLAR

The **BUCKLE COLLAR** is the standard collar used for everyday purposes. Be sure that you adjust the buckle on growing puppies. Check it every day. It can become too tight overnight! These collars can be made of leather or nylon. Attach your dog's identification tags to this collar.

The **CHOKE COLLAR** is designed for training. It is constructed of highly polished steel so that it slides easily through the stainless steel loop. The idea is that the dog controls the pressure around his neck and he will stop pulling if the collar becomes uncomfortable. It should *not* be used on heavily coated breeds like the Spanish Water Dog.

The **HALTER** is for a trained dog that has to be restrained to prevent running away, chasing a cat and the like. Considered the most humane of all collars, it is frequently used on smaller dogs on which collars are not comfortable.

Ready or not—here's Sebastian, owned by Barry and Marlene Duke.

Your local pet shop will have a variety of food and water bowls. Choose durable, easily cleaned bowls for your Spanish Water Dog.

PHOTO COURTESY OF MIKKI PET PRODUCTS.

partition a room, etc. These things will vary depending on your situation, but it is important that you have everything you need to feed and make your Spanish Water Dog comfortable in his first few days at home.

PUPPY-PROOFING YOUR HOME

Aside from making sure that your Spanish Water Dog will be comfortable in your home, you also have to make sure that your home is safe for your Spanish Water Dog. This means taking precautions that your pup will not get into anything he should not get into and that there is nothing within his reach that may harm him should he sniff it, chew it, inspect it, etc. This probably seems obvious since, while you are primarily concerned with your pup's safety, at the same time you do not want your belongings to be ruined. Breakables should be placed out of reach if your dog is to have full run of the house. If he is to be limited to certain places within the house, keep any potentially dangerous items in the "off-limits" areas.

An electrical cord can pose a danger should the puppy decide to taste it—and who is going to convince a pup that it would not make a great chew toy? Cords should be fastened tightly against the wall and kept from puppy teeth. If your dog is going to spend time in a crate, make sure that there is nothing near his crate that he can reach if he sticks his curious little nose or paws through the openings. Just as you would with a child, keep all household cleaners and chemicals where the pup cannot reach them.

It is also important to make sure that the outside of your home is safe. Of course, your puppy should never be unsupervised, but a pup let loose on your fenced property will want to run and

Though no dog owner's favorite chore, you should always clean up after your dog has relieved himself. Fortunately, you can purchase tools to aid in the cleanup task.

explore, and he should be granted that freedom. Do not let a fence give you a false sense of security. If not given enough exercise and activity, your Spanish Water Dog will devise clever ways of escaping and running away, including digging, climbing and jumping. Remember how agile and bright this dog is! Don't believe for a Madrid minute that an average-height fence will deter the Spanish Water Dog if he feels there is good need for his being on the other side. A safe fence should be no less than 5–6 feet (152–182 cm) high and well embedded into the ground. Be sure to repair or secure any gaps in the fence. Check the fence periodically to ensure that it is in good shape and make repairs as needed; a very

CHEMICAL TOXINS
Scour your garage for potential puppy dangers. Remove weed killers, pesticides and antifreeze materials. Antifreeze is highly toxic and just a few drops can kill a puppy or an adult dog. The sweet taste attracts the animal, who will quickly consume it from the floor or pavement.

What could be more irresistible than an eight-week-old Spanish Water Dog invading your home? Don't give up your whole *casa* too fast!

determined pup may return to the same spot to "work on it" until he is able to get through or over.

FIRST TRIP TO THE VET

You have selected your puppy, and your home and family are ready. Now all you have to do is collect your Spanish Water Dog from the breeder and the fun begins, right? Well...not so fast. Something else you need to plan is your pup's first trip to the vet. Perhaps the breeder can recommend someone in the area who knows working or herding dogs, or maybe you know some other owners who can suggest a good vet. Either way, you should have

an appointment arranged for your pup before you pick him up.

The pup's first visit will consist of an overall examination to make sure that the pup does not have any problems that are not apparent to you. The vet will also set up a schedule for the pup's vaccinations; the breeder will inform you of which ones the pup has already received and the vet can continue from there.

INTRODUCTION TO THE FAMILY

Everyone in the house will be excited about the puppy's coming home and will want to pet him and play with him, but it is best to make the introduction low-key so as not to overwhelm the puppy. He is apprehensive already. It is the first time he has been separated from his mother and the breeder, and the ride to your home is likely to be the first time he has been in a car. The last thing you want to do is smother him, as this will only frighten him further. This is not to say that human contact is not extremely necessary at this stage, because this is the time when a connection between the pup and his human family is formed. Gentle petting and soothing words should help console the pup, as well as just putting him down and letting him explore on his own (under your watchful eye, of course).

The pup may approach the family members or may busy himself with exploring for a while. Gradually, each person should spend some time with the pup, one at a time, crouching down to get as close to the pup's level as possible, letting him sniff their hands and petting him gently. He definitely needs human attention and he needs to be touched—this is how to form an immediate bond. Just remember that the pup is experiencing many things for the first time, at the same time. There are new people, new noises, new smells and new things to investigate, so be gentle, be affectionate and be as comforting as you can be.

PUP'S FIRST NIGHT HOME

You have traveled home with your new charge safely in his crate. He's been to the vet for a thorough check-up; he's been weighed, his papers have been examined and perhaps he's even been vaccinated and wormed as well. He's met the whole family, including the excited children and the less-than-happy cat. He's explored his area, his new bed, the yard and anywhere else he's been permitted. He's eaten his first meal at home and relieved himself in the proper place. He's heard lots of new sounds, smelled new friends and seen more of the outside world than ever before... and that was just the first day!

He's worn out and is ready for bed...or so you think!

It's puppy's first night home and you are ready to say "Good night." Keep in mind that this is his first night ever to be sleeping alone. His dam and littermates are no longer at paw's length and he's a bit scared, cold and lonely. Be reassuring to your new family

FEEDING TIPS

You will probably start feeding your pup the same food that he has been getting from the breeder; the breeder should give you a few days' supply to start you off. Although you should not give your pup too many treats, you will want to have puppy treats on hand for coaxing, training, rewards, etc. Be careful, though, as a small pup's calorie requirements are relatively low and a few treats can add up to almost a full day's worth of calories without the required nutrition.

member, but this is not the time to spoil him and give in to his inevitable whining.

Puppies whine. They whine to let others know where they are and hopefully to get company out of it. At bedtime, place your pup in his new bed or crate in his designated area. Mercifully, he may fall asleep without a peep. When the inevitable occurs, however, ignore the whining—he is fine. Be strong and keep his best interest in mind. Do not allow yourself to feel guilty and

---

IN DUE TIME

It will take at least two weeks for your puppy to become accustomed to his new surroundings. Give him lots of love, attention, handling, frequent opportunities to relieve himself, a diet he likes to eat and a place he can call his own.

---

visit the pup. He will fall asleep eventually.

Many breeders recommend placing a piece of bedding from the pup's former home in his new bed so that he recognizes and is comforted by the scent of his littermates. Others still advise placing a hot water bottle in the bed for warmth. The latter may be a good idea, provided the pup doesn't attempt to suckle—he'll get good and wet, and may not fall asleep so fast.

Puppy's first night can be somewhat stressful for both the pup and his new family. Remember that you are setting the tone of nighttime at your house. Unless you want to play with your pup every night at 10 p.m., midnight and 2 a.m., don't initiate the habit. Your family will thank you, and eventually so will your pup!

PREVENTING PUPPY PROBLEMS

SOCIALIZATION

Now that you have done all of the preparatory work and have helped your pup get accustomed to his new home and family, it is about time for you to have some fun! Socializing your Spanish Water Dog pup gives you the opportunity to show off your new friend—likely you are the first person in your neighborhood with such an astounding rare breed—and your pup gets to reap the benefits of

A bitch pup and a dog pup, enjoying a romp in the great outdoors. Socialization begins with littermates and then continues with your family.

being an adorable woolly creature that people will want to pet and, in general, think is absolutely precious!

Besides getting to know his new family, your puppy should be exposed to other people, animals and situations. This will help him become well adjusted as he grows up and less prone to being timid or fearful of the new things he will encounter. Of course, he must not come into close contact with dogs you don't know well until his course of injections is fully complete.

Your pup's socialization began with the breeder, but now it is your responsibility to continue it. The socialization he receives until the age of 12 weeks is the most critical, as this is the time when he forms his impressions of the outside world. Be especially careful during the eight-to-ten-week-

old period, also known as the fear period. The interaction he receives during this time should be gentle and reassuring. Lack of socialization, and/or negative experiences during the socialization period, can manifest itself in fear and aggression as the dog grows up. Your puppy needs lots of positive interaction, which of course includes human contact, affection, handling and exposure to other animals.

Once your pup has received his necessary vaccinations, feel free to take him out and about (on his leash, of course). Walk him around the neighborhood, take him on your daily errands, let people pet him, let him meet other dogs and pets, etc. Puppies do not have to try to make friends; there will be no shortage of people who will want to introduce themselves to your beguiling

PROPER SOCIALIZATION

The socialization period for puppies is from age 8 to 16 weeks. This is the time when puppies need to leave their birth family and take up residence with their new owners, where they will meet many new people, other pets, etc. Failure to be adequately socialized can cause the dog to grow up fearing others and being shy and unfriendly due to a lack of self-confidence.

an excited child can unintentionally handle a pup too roughly, or an overzealous pup can playfully nip a little too hard. You want to make socialization experiences positive ones. What a pup learns during this very formative stage will affect his attitude toward future encounters. You want your dog to be comfortable around everyone. A pup that has a bad experience with a child may grow up to be a dog that is shy around or aggressive toward children.

CONSISTENCY IN TRAINING

Dogs, being pack animals, naturally need a leader, or else they try to establish dominance in their packs. When you welcome a dog into your family, the choice of who becomes the leader and who becomes the "pack" is entirely up to you! Your pup's intuitive quest for dominance, coupled with the fact that it is nearly impossible to look at an adorable Spanish Water Dog pup and not cave in, give the pup almost an unfair advantage in getting the upper hand! A pup will definitely test the waters to see what he can and cannot do. Do not give in to that pleading expression—stand your ground when it comes to disciplining the pup and make sure that all family members do the same. It will only confuse the pup if Mother tells him to get off the sofa when he is used to sitting up there with Father to watch the

curly puppy. Just make sure that you carefully supervise each meeting. If the neighborhood children want to say hello, for example, that is great—children and pups most often make great companions. However, sometimes

nightly news. Avoid discrepancies by having all members of the household decide on the rules before the pup even comes home...and be consistent in enforcing them! Early training shapes the dog's personality, so you cannot be unclear in what you expect.

COMMON PUPPY PROBLEMS

The best way to prevent puppy problems is to be proactive in stopping an undesirable behavior as soon as it starts. The old saying "You can't teach an old dog new tricks" does not necessarily hold true, but it *is* true that it is much easier to discourage bad behavior in a young developing pup than to wait until the pup's bad behavior becomes the adult dog's bad habit. There are some problems that are especially prevalent in puppies as they develop.

NIPPING

As puppies start to teethe, they feel the need to sink their teeth into anything available...unfortunately, that usually includes your fingers, arms, hair and toes. You may find this behavior cute for the first five seconds...until you feel just how sharp those puppy teeth are. Nipping is something you want to discourage immediately and consistently with a firm "No!" (or whatever number of firm "Nos" it takes for him to understand that you mean business). Then, replace your finger with an appropriate chew toy.

While nipping behavior is merely annoying when the dog is young, it can become dangerous

Providing your puppy with chew toys, and praising him for using them, will divert his considerable chewing energy into safe, rather than dangerous or destructive, behavior.

as your Spanish Water Dog's adult teeth grow in and his jaws develop, and he continues to think it is okay to gnaw on human appendages. Your Spanish Water Dog does not mean any harm with a friendly nip, but he also does not know his own strength.

CRYING/WHINING

Your pup will often cry, whine, whimper, howl or make some type of commotion when he is left alone. This is basically his way of calling out for attention to make sure that you know he is there and that you have not forgotten about him. Your puppy feels inse-

---

MANNERS MATTER

During the socialization process, a puppy should meet people, experience different environments and definitely be exposed to other canines. Through playing and interacting with other dogs, your puppy will learn lessons, ranging from controlling the pressure of his jaws by biting his littermates to the inner-workings of the canine pack that he will apply to his human relationships for the rest of his life. That is why removing a puppy from his litter too early (before eight weeks) can be detrimental to the pup's development.

With proper introductions and training, your Spanish Water Dog will accept other dogs as family members. This *perro* and his Pomeranian pal get along famously.

cure when he is left alone, when you are out of the house and he is in his crate or when you are in another part of the house and he cannot see you. The noise he is making is an expression of the anxiety he feels at being alone, so he needs to be taught that being alone is okay. You are not actually training the dog to stop making noise; rather, you are training him to feel comfortable when he is alone and thus removing the need for him to make the noise.

This is where the crate with cozy bedding and a toy comes in handy. You want to know that your pup is safe when you are not there to supervise, and you know that he will be safe in his crate rather than roaming freely about the house. In order for the pup to stay in his crate without making a fuss, he first needs to be comfort-

able in his crate. On that note, it is extremely important that the crate is never used as a form of punishment; this will cause the pup to view the crate as a negative place, rather than as a place of his own for safety and retreat.

Accustom the pup to the crate in short, gradually increasing time intervals in which you put him in the crate, maybe with a treat, and stay in the room with him. If he cries or makes a fuss, do not go to him, but stay in his sight. Gradually he will realize that staying in his crate is okay without your help, and it will not be so traumatic for him when you are not around. You may want to leave the radio on softly when you leave the house; the sound of human voices may be comforting to him.

CHEWING TIPS

Chewing goes hand in hand with nipping in the sense that a teething puppy is always looking for a way to soothe his aching gums. In this case, instead of chewing on you, he may have taken a liking to your favorite shoe or something else that he should not be chewing. Again, realize that this is a normal canine behavior that does not need to be discouraged, only redirected. Your pup just needs to be taught what is acceptable to chew on and what is off-limits. Consistently tell him "No!" when you catch him chewing on something forbidden and give him a chew toy.

Conversely, praise him when you catch him chewing on something appropriate. In this way, you are discouraging the inappropriate behavior and reinforcing the desired behavior. The puppy's chewing should stop after his adult teeth have come in, but an adult dog continues to chew for various reasons—perhaps because he is bored, needs to relieve tension or just likes to chew. That is why it is important to redirect his chewing when he is still young.

FEEDING YOUR SPANISH WATER DOG

Given the rudimentary existence that most Spanish Water Dogs have endured until recently, this dog is perhaps the least demanding of all when it comes to feeding. His recent ancestors accompanied shepherds and fishermen, who traditionally fed them on dry bread and leftovers. In spite of this scarce diet, the dogs never seemed to go hungry. The Spanish Water Dog is a survivor, and during his working hours he also hunted small animals—rabbit, birds and fish—that he would catch in the fields or in the water. That is, until recently, the Spanish Water Dog survived in the same way that dogs existed when they accompanied primitive humans in our remote past.

Life in the 21st century is considerably more complex than tossing our Spanish Water Dog a stray rabbit or fluke! The pet industry has provided us with many options for our pure-bred dogs (and other dogs, too!), much of which can be very overwhelming. Merely choosing between dry, semi-dry and moist foods can be quite a decision. Likewise, many dog breeders resist many commercial packaged foods because they contain chemical additives and preservatives. The natural Spanish Water Dog certainly hasn't developed such a strong resistance to disease from absorbing so many chemicals in his diet!

STORING DOG FOOD

You must store your dry dog food carefully. Open packages of dog food quickly lose their vitamin value, usually within 90 days of being opened. Mold spores and vermin could also contaminate the food.

Thus, my recommendation is to offer your dog a prepared dog food as the basis of his diet, and supplement it with fresh and raw food. He should have meat, mainly beef, chicken or rabbit, fish, vegetables and eggs. Fruit should be offered, though not with the regular meal, as they are digested and metabolized in a different way. The puppy should also eat high-fiber bread regularly. A fresh diet will be more costly and time-consuming, but with planning and smart shopping, it is very affordable and your dog will look and act healthier.

My advice would be two meals a day, one of dry dog food and the other of fresh food. Such a diet benefits the dog in many ways:

- Diminished water intake (dry food makes dogs drink more water than natural food);
- Better digestion (as natural food is digester faster than processed foods);
- Better nutrition (since natural foods have a higher level of proteins, vitamins and minerals);
- Diminished urination and defecation (as the body makes better use of natural food).

EXERCISE FOR YOUR SPANISH WATER DOG

One of the most obvious characteristics of the breed is its vivacity, agility and energy; therefore, we cannot condemn him to a lazy life of inactivity. The Spanish Water Dog likes to run and enjoy great open fields like his ancestors have done for thousands of years. Thus, it is vital that Spanish Water Dogs who are pets (and/or show dogs) be given ample

The breeder begins the weaning process around four weeks, alternating between nursing and meals fed from a bowl.

GRAIN-BASED DIETS

Some less expensive dog foods are based on grains and other plant proteins. While these products may appear to be attractively priced, many breeders prefer a diet based on animal proteins and believe that they are more conducive to your dog's health. Many grain-based diets rely on soy protein, which may cause flatulence (passing gas).

There are many cases, however, when your dog might require a special diet. These special requirements should only be recommended by your vet.

Don't overlook the "water" in your dog's name. Nothing proves better exercise (or more fun!) than a romp in the ocean with a Perro de Agua *amigo*.

excellent duck retriever in lakes and swamps. As a hunter, he is fearless at getting into thick brush to catch rabbits, tracking them down with his nose to the ground, his heart not beating for as long as necessary until he locates his quarry.

The Spanish Water Dog needs to be active many hours a day to be happy. If not given ample exercise on a daily basis. The clever owner will devise many ways for the dog to release his energy, whether in agility exercises, working about the home and farm, running with sheep or other dogs, hunting, herding, etc! Organized classes for obedience and agility training are ideal for dogs who live in suburbs or cities, where vast expanses of land are not available.

Don't overlook the "water" in your dog's name! Any chance the dog has to show off his natural ability in the water—whether a brook, lake, ocean or backyard pool—your Spanish Water Dog will revel in the chance to hit the *agua*! You will be amazed at how naturally this dog swims and dives. In the northern region of Spain, the breed is called the "Fishing Dog," and dogs are trained to dive from the sides of boats or docks to retrieve fish that escape from the fisherman's net. The Fishing Dog also is an

THE CANINE GOURMET

Your dog does not prefer a fresh bone. Indeed, he wants it properly aged and, if given such a treat indoors, he is more likely to try to bury it in the carpet than he is to settle in for a good chew! If you have a fenced yard, give him such delicacies outside and guide him to a place suitable for his "bone yard." He will carefully place the treasure in its earthy vault and seemingly forget about it. Trust me, his seeming distaste or lack of thanks for your thoughtfulness is not that at all. He will return in a few days to inspect the bone, perhaps to re-bury it, and, when it is just right, he will relish it as much as you do that cooked-to-perfection steak. If he is in a concrete or bricked kennel run, he will be especially frustrated at the hopelessness of the situation. He will vacillate between ignoring it completely, giving it a few licks to speed the curing process with saliva and trying to hide it behind the water bowl! When the bone has aged a bit, he will set to work on it.

cise, this is a restless house dog who will seek out "duties" on his own. The dog enjoys playing with all members of his human family, which significantly improves his capacity for understanding and enhances his bond with the pack. He is loud and playful, and that makes him an excellent partner for children—who frequently tire of playing before he does.

GROOMING AND COAT CARE
First of all, this is a dog that has wool instead of hair; thus, his grooming requirements are vastly different than those of an "ordinary" dog. At birth, the Spanish Water Dog's coat is a very thin, weak wool, which implies that, around the age of three months, the puppy has to be sheared. Later on, the wool will grow stronger and of better quality. This new wool will begin to grow and take shape at five or six months of age.

Unlike other breeds who have such resilient, full coats, sculpting is not permitted for the Spanish Water Dog. Therefore, it is essential to untangle knots daily with your fingers, always working from the outside to the inside, giving the coat the desired curly, somewhat tousled appearance.

When allowed to grow long, the curly wool forms cords, similar to those of the Puli, and these require maintenance to keep from causing the dog discomfort. If the cords are not cared for, they will form mats and, in cases of poor maintenance, restrict the dog's movement. For healthy skin and coat, the cords must be left open to the skin so that air can circulate properly. Different fanciers keep the coat at different lengths. The recommended maximum

EXERCISE ALERT!
You should be careful where you exercise your dog. Many areas have been sprayed with chemicals that are highly toxic to both dogs and humans. Never allow your dog to eat grass or drink from puddles on either public or private grounds, as the run-off water may contain chemicals from sprays and herbicides.

the hair falling over the dog's face, eyes and feet is also cut. It is done whenever necessary and regularly at the end of the year to stop spikes, seeds or thorns from becoming entangled in the wool, and also to help the dog see better.

When grooming the dog, it is important to take into account the environment in which the dog lives as well as his working conditions. If the dogs are used as pets rather than as working dogs and if they live inside the home with their human families, it is then

LET THE SUN SHINE

Your dog needs daily sunshine for the same reason people do. Pets kept inside homes with curtains drawn against the sun suffer from "SAD" (Seasonal Affected Disorder) to the same degree as humans. We now know that sunlight must enter the iris and thus progress to the pineal gland to regulate the body's hormonal system. When we live and work in artificial light, both circadian rhythms and hormone balances are disturbed.

length of the hair for show dogs is 4.7 inches (12 cm), 5.9 inches (15 cm) extending the curl, and the ideal minimum is 1.2 inches (3 cm).

It is advisable to shear the dog once a year, as shepherds still do today, coinciding with the same time of year that the sheep are sheared. In some areas of Spain, more appropriate to shear them twice a year (for instance, in April and September), when the weather is warm. Fleas can be unbearable in the hot months, and the sheared dog is less prone to infestation and having the parasites ruin his lovely wool.

By and large, this dog does not require excessive grooming. Baths should be given about every two weeks, especially if the dog is living inside the house. Bathing a Spanish Water Dog feels like washing a thick woolly sweater, if I do say so! It is necessary to first

SOAP IT UP

The use of human soap products like shampoo, bubble bath and hand soap can be damaging to a dog's coat and skin. Human products are too strong; they remove the protective oils coating the dog's hair and skin that make him water-resistant. Use only a mild shampoo made especially for dogs. Swimming will also help keep the Spanish Water Dog's coat clean and properly pH-balanced.

A close-up of the unique texture of the coat in its curly (pre-cord) state.

wet the coat with warm water, but never with excessively hot water, since this would make the wool harden. Pour water abundantly from top to bottom and down the sides of the body to make sure it gets down to the very skin.

The pet Spanish Water Dog is commonly maintained in a short, manageable coat. This is achieved most easily with an electric clipper.

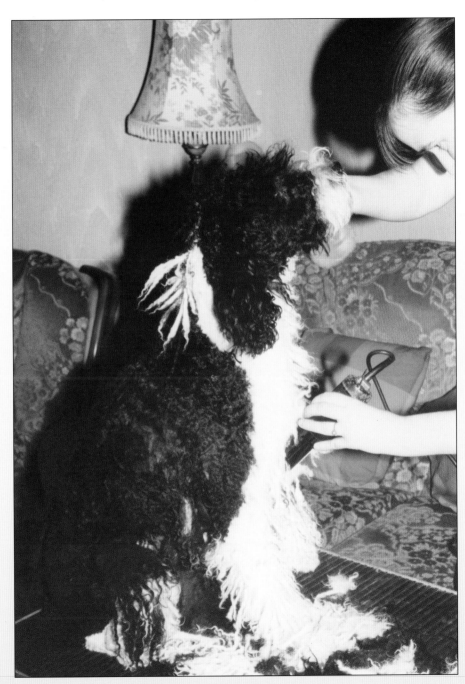

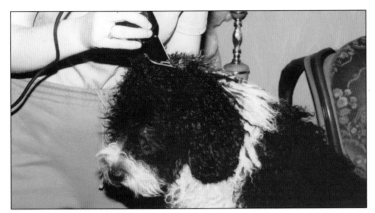

A well-trained dog, who has been acclimated to the electric trimmer from an early age, stands quietly while his coat is being trimmed.

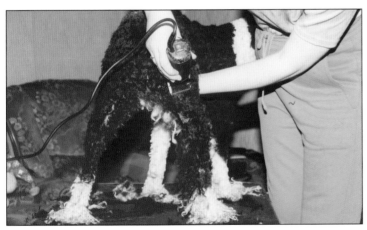

Having a grooming table with a non-skid top makes the task of grooming much simpler and safer.

The dog's coat is sheared annually to remove all the dog's wool as well as to rid the coat of burrs and mats.

The ears must be trimmed with scissors. Be very careful that you do not cut the ear leather. This can be assured by holding the wool in your fingers and cutting as shown here.

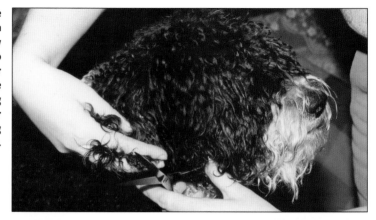

The feet are tidied up by trimming around the edges with the scissors.

The puppy or summer clip, after all those glorious curls have been trimmed away.

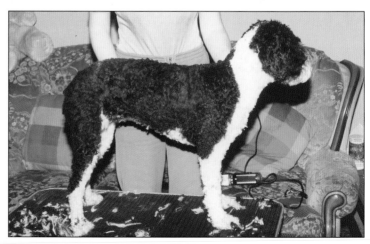

Reasonably enough, if you do not want the coat to tangle, you should never lather the shampoo by rubbing the wool in circles. Do not overuse shampoo on the Perro de Agua, and only use a neutral shampoo that will not affect the pH of the dog's skin. The dog needs his natural oils to protect him from cold water and inclement weather. Likewise, the dog whose skin lacks its natural protection can develop disagreeable doggy odor or possibly develop moist dermatitis (or hot spots).

Brushes and combs are not recommended. Again, the use of such implements risks altering the quality of the dog's woolly curls, which are one of the most celebrated characteristics of this breed. Yet, hair drying is very important. If the cords are not properly dried, they can become mildewed and attract dirt and other debris. If the dog lives in a wet, cold area, it will be necessary to use a hand dryer at medium-soft level to keep him from catching a cold. Blow drying the coat can take a few hours, given the nature of the dog's wool. However, if the dog lives in a warm area, it is fine for him to dry naturally in the sun; it may take a couple of days for him to dry completely.

Do these grooming details make the Spanish Water Dog sound involved and complicated?

THE "WOOLITE" TREATMENT

This breed is shown from clipped (minimum of 3 cm) to full-corded coat (maximum 12 cm), but the coat length must be uniform all over. The puppies are clipped at an early age (approximately 4 months) with a no. 5 blade or an equivalent to assist in coat growth; it also stops matting in the soft puppy coat. The dogs must be clipped at least once a year.

Brushes and combs are never used on this breed, as it is swimming in clean water that keeps the coat in good condition and helps to separate the cords. When bathed, the coat must be treated like a fine wool sweater—the water should be tepid and the shampoo mild and diluted. All shampoo residue must be washed carefully from the coat. It is better to let the dogs swim regularly (at least once every two weeks) or else the shampoo will strip the coat of its natural oils.

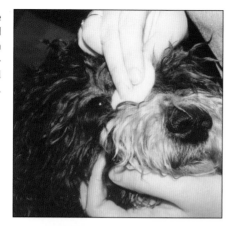

Tear stains are easily removed with a soft cotton ball and tear-stain-removal solution.

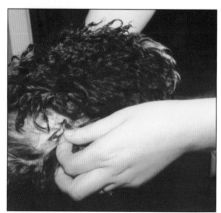

Long hairs in the ear are easily and painlessly removed by carefully plucking.

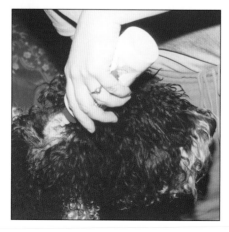

The ear is cleaned with a soft cotton ball and ear-cleaning solution or powder made for dogs.

Actually, no! You simply must know about this dog's unique coat before attempting to bring a Perro de Agua Español into your home. The woolly coat has a distinct advantage that is enjoyed by few in the dog fraternity. Spanish Water Dogs do not shed annually as most breeds do, which means that, once you have learned to deal with the wool, you will have an extraordinarily clean animal at home.

EYE AND EAR CARE

Regarding care of the eyes and ears, they usually get dirty since they are covered in wool. You should clean the eyes daily to remove any tears or discharge that tends to accumulate in and around the tear ducts. The ideal is to use a cotton ball with warm water and to

NAIL FILING

You can purchase an electric tool to grind down a dog's nails rather than cut them. Some dogs don't seem to mind the electric grinder but will object strongly to nail clippers. Judging your own dog's reactions will help you make the right choice.

do it at the beginning of the day. Likewise, it is wise to inspect the inside of the ears every week and remove any wax or debris that accumulates there. You may want to use some olive oil on a cotton ball, or perhaps an ear cleanser that you buy at your pet shop. If your dog swims frequently, you should check his ears every two or three days. Likewise, it is advisable to check the ears more frequently in the warm months.

NAIL TRIMMING

Grooming time is a good time to accustom your Spanish Water Dog to having his nails trimmed and feet inspected. Always inspect your dog's feet for cracked pads. Check between the toes for splinters and thorns that may be embedded in the soft hair between the pads and toes. Pay particular attention to any swollen or tender areas.

I suggest attending to your dog's nails at intervals of about every three weeks and certainly no longer than four weeks. Long nails spread and weaken the foot. The nails of a dog that isn't exercising on rough terrain will grow long very quickly.

Each nail has a blood vessel running through the center called the "quick." The quick grows close to the end of the nail and contains very sensitive nerve endings. If the nail is allowed to grow too long, it will be impossi-

PEDICURE TIP
A dog that spends a lot of time outside on a hard surface, such as cement or pavement, will have his nails naturally worn down and may not need to have them trimmed as often, except maybe in the colder months when he is not outside as much. Regardless, it is best to get your dog accustomed to the nail-trimming procedure at an early age so that he is used to it. Some dogs are especially sensitive about having their feet touched, but if a dog has experienced it since puppyhood, it should not bother him.

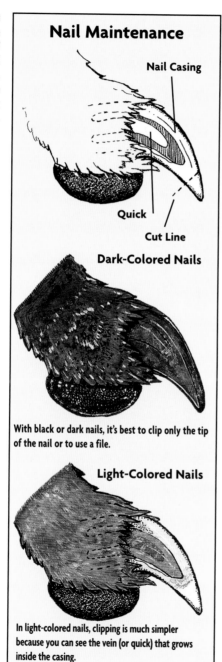

Nail Maintenance

Nail Casing

Quick

Cut Line

Dark-Colored Nails

With black or dark nails, it's best to clip only the tip of the nail or to use a file.

Light-Colored Nails

In light-colored nails, clipping is much simpler because you can see the vein (or quick) that grows inside the casing.

ble to cut it back to a proper length without cutting into the quick. This causes severe pain to the dog and can also result in a great deal of bleeding that can be very difficult to stop.

Nails can be trimmed with canine nail clippers or an electric nail grinder called a drummel. Use the "fine" grinding disc on the drummel, because this allows you to trim back the nail a little bit at a time, practically eliminating the risk of any bleeding.

Always proceed with caution and remove only a small portion of the nail at a time. Should the quick be nipped in the trimming process, there are any number of blood-clotting products available at pet shops that will almost immediately stem the flow of blood. You can also use a styptic pencil, such as the type used for shaving. It is wise to have one of these products on hand in case your dog breaks a nail in some way.

TRAVELING WITH YOUR DOG

CAR TRAVEL

You should accustom your Spanish Water Dog to riding in a car at an early age. You may or may not take him in the car often, but at the very least he will need to go to the vet and you do not want these trips to be traumatic for the dog or troublesome for you. The safest way for a dog to ride in the car is in his crate. If he uses a crate in the house, you can use the same crate for travel.

Another option for car travel is a specially made safety harness for dogs, which straps the dog in much like a seat belt. Do not let the dog roam loose in the vehicle—this is very dangerous! If you should stop short, your dog can be thrown and injured. If the dog starts climbing on you and pestering you while you are driving, you will not be able to concen-

trate on the road. It is an unsafe situation for everyone—human and canine.

For long trips, be prepared to stop to let the dog relieve himself. Take with you whatever you need to clean up after him, including some paper kitchen towels and perhaps some old toweling for use should he have a toileting accident in the car or suffer from motion sickness.

Your Spanish Water Dog should always travel in his crate. Never let him have the run of the van while you're driving.

> **TRAVEL ALERT**
> When you travel with your dog, it's a good idea to take along water from home or to buy bottled water for the trip. In areas where water is sometimes chemically treated and sometimes comes right out of the ground, you can prevent adverse reactions to this essential part of your dog's diet.

AIR TRAVEL

Contact your chosen airline before proceeding with travel plans that include your Spanish Water Dog. The dog will be required to travel in a fiberglass crate and you must adhere to the airline's specifications for the crate's type, size and labeling. To help put the dog at ease, give him one of his favorite toys in the crate. Do not feed the dog for several hours before checking in for your flight so that you minimize his need to relieve himself; a light meal is best. Certain regulations require you to provide documentation of when the dog has last been fed.

Make sure your dog is properly identified and that your contact information appears on his ID tags and on his crate. Except for small pets and very small dogs, animals travel in a different area of the plane than human passengers, so every rule must be strictly followed so as to prevent the risk of getting separated from your Spanish Water Dog.

BOARDING

So you want to take a family trip—and you want to include *all* members of the family. You would probably make arrangements for accommodations ahead of time anyway, but this is especially important when traveling with a dog. You do not want to make an overnight stop at the only place around for miles, only to find out that they do not allow dogs. Also, you do not want to reserve a place for your family without confirming that you are traveling with a dog, because, if it is against their policy, you may end up without a place to stay.

TRAVEL TIP

Never leave your dog alone in the car. In hot weather, your dog can die from the high temperature inside a closed vehicle; even a car parked in the shade can heat up very quickly. Leaving the window open is dangerous as well since the dog can hurt himself trying to get out.

Alternatively, if you are traveling and choose not to bring your Spanish Water Dog, you will have to make arrangements for him while you are away. Some options are to take him to a neighbor's house to stay while you are gone, to have a trusted neighbor stay at your house or to bring your dog to a reputable boarding kennel. If you choose to board him at a kennel, you should visit in advance to see the facilities provided and where the dogs are kept. Are the dogs' areas spacious and kept clean? Talk to some of the employees and observe how they treat the dogs—do they spend time with the dogs, play with them, groom them, exercise them, etc.? Also find out the kennel's policy on vaccinations and what they require. This is for all of the dogs' safety, since there is a greater risk of diseases being passed from dog to dog when dogs are kept together.

Should you decide not to take your dog on vacation with you, select a boarding facility that is well kept and run by exceptionally nice, caring dog people.

IDENTIFICATION

Your Spanish Water Dog is your valued companion and friend. That is why you always keep a close eye on him and you have made sure that he cannot escape from the yard or wriggle out of his collar and run away from you. However, accidents can happen and there may come a time when your dog unexpectedly becomes separated from you. If this unfortunate event should occur, the first thing on your mind will be finding him. Proper identification, including an ID tag, and possibly a tattoo and/or a microchip, will increase the chances of his being returned to you safely and quickly.

Proper identification tags are a simple way to help ensure that you will be able to retrieve your dog should he wander away from home.

TRAINING YOUR
SPANISH WATER DOG

Living with an untrained dog is a lot like owning a piano that you do not know how to play—it is a nice object to look at, but it does not do much more than that to bring you pleasure. Now try taking piano lessons, and suddenly the piano comes alive and brings forth magical sounds and rhythms that set your heart singing and your body swaying.

The same is true with your Spanish Water Dog. Any dog is a big responsibility and, if not trained sensibly, may develop unacceptable behavior that annoys you or could even cause family friction. An untrained

Training your dog means encouraging him to do the right thing. When teaching commands, you must start off by showing the dog what is expected.

> **PARENTAL GUIDANCE**
> Training a dog is a life experience. Many parents admit that much of what they know about raising children they learned from caring for their dogs. Dogs respond to love, fairness and guidance, just as children do. Become a good dog owner and you may become an even better parent.

Spanish Water Dog can resort to engaging in destructive behaviors to release his considerable energy.

To train your Spanish Water Dog, you may like to enroll in an obedience class. Teach your dog good manners as you learn how and why he behaves the way he does. Find out how to communicate with your dog and how to recognize and understand his communications with you. Suddenly the dog takes on a new role in your life—he is clever, interesting, well behaved and fun to be with. He demonstrates his bond of devotion to you daily. In other words, your Spanish Water Dog does wonders for your ego because he constantly reminds you that you are not only his leader, you are his hero!

Those involved with teaching dog obedience and counseling owners about their dogs' behavior have discovered some interesting facts about dog ownership. For example, training dogs when they are puppies results in the highest rate of success in developing well-mannered and well-adjusted adult dogs. Training an older dog, from six months to six years of age, can produce almost equal results, providing that the owner accepts the dog's slower rate of learning capability and is willing to work patiently to help the dog succeed at developing to his fullest potential. Unfortunately, many owners of untrained adult dogs lack the patience factor, so they do not persist until their dogs are successful at learning particular behaviors.

Training a puppy aged 10 to 16 weeks (20 weeks at the most) is like working with a dry sponge in a pool of water. The pup soaks up whatever you show him and constantly looks for more things to do and learn. At this early age, his body is not yet producing hormones, and therein lies the reason for such a high rate of success. Without hormones, he is focused on his owners and not particularly interested in investigating other places, dogs, people, etc. You are his leader: his provider of food, water, shelter and security. He latches onto you

REAP THE REWARDS

If you start with a normal, healthy dog and give him time, patience and some carefully executed lessons, you will reap the rewards of that training for the life of the dog. And what a life it will be! The two of you will find immeasurable pleasure in the companionship you have built together with love, respect and understanding.

Young pups are "clean slates" upon which you inprint the picture of appropriate behavior and good manners.

and wants to stay close. He will usually follow you from room to room, will not let you out of his sight when you are outdoors with him and will respond in like manner to the people and animals you encounter. If you greet a friend warmly, your dog will be happy to greet the person as well. If, however, you are hesitant or anxious about the approach of a stranger, he will respond to the person accordingly.

Once the puppy begins to produce hormones, his natural curiosity emerges and he begins to investigate the world around him. It is at this time when you may notice that the untrained dog begins to wander away from you and even ignore your commands to stay close. When this behavior becomes a problem, you have two choices: get rid of the dog or train him. It is strongly urged that you choose the latter option.

You usually will be able to find obedience classes within a reasonable distance from your home, but you can also do a lot to train your dog yourself. Sometimes there are classes available, but the tuition is too costly. Whatever the circumstances, the solution to training your dog without formal classes lies within the pages of this book.

This chapter is devoted to helping you train your Spanish Water Dog at home. If the recommended procedures are followed faithfully, you may expect positive results that will prove rewarding both to you and your dog.

TRAINING RULES

If you want to be successful in training your dog, you have four rules to obey yourself:

1. Develop an understanding of how a dog thinks.
2. Do not blame the dog for lack of communication.
3. Define your dog's personality and act accordingly.
4. Have patience and be consistent.

Whether your new charge is a puppy or a mature adult, the methods of teaching and the techniques we use in training basic behaviors are the same. After all, no dog, whether puppy or adult, likes harsh or inhumane methods. All creatures, however, respond favorably to gentle motivational methods and sincere praise and encouragement. Now let us get started.

HOUSE-TRAINING

You can train a puppy to relieve himself wherever you choose, but this must be somewhere suitable. You should bear in mind from the outset that when your puppy is old enough to go out in public places, any canine deposits must be removed at once. You will always have to carry with you a small plastic bag or "poop-scoop."

Outdoor training includes such surfaces as grass, soil and cement. Indoor training usually means training your dog to newspaper. When deciding on the surface and location that you will want your Spanish Water Dog to use, be sure it is going to be permanent. Training your dog to grass and then changing your mind a few months later is extremely difficult for both dog and owner.

Next, choose the command you will use each and every time you want your puppy to void. "Hurry up" and "Let's go" are

CALM DOWN
Dogs will do anything for your attention. If you reward the dog when he is calm and attentive, you will develop a well-mannered dog. If, on the other hand, you greet your dog excitedly and encourage him to wrestle with you, the dog will greet you the same way and you will have a hyperactive dog on your hands.

PRACTICE MAKES PERFECT!

- Have training lessons with your dog every day in several short segments—three to five times a day for a few minutes at a time is ideal.
- Do not have long practice sessions. The dog will become easily bored.
- Never practice when you are tired, ill, worried or in an otherwise negative mood. This will transmit to the dog and may have an adverse effect on his performance.

  Think fun, short and above all *positive!* End each session on a high note, rather than a failed exercise, and make sure to give a lot of praise. Enjoy the training and help your dog enjoy it, too.

examples of commands commonly used by dog owners. Get in the habit of giving the puppy your chosen relief command before you take him out. That way, when he becomes an adult, you will be able to determine if he wants to go out when you ask him. A confirmation will be signs of interest, such as wagging his tail, watching you intently, going to the door, etc.

PUPPY'S NEEDS

The puppy needs to relieve himself after play periods, after each meal, after he has been sleeping and at any time he indicates that he is looking for a place to urinate or defecate. The urinary and intestinal tract muscles of very young puppies are not fully developed. Therefore, like human babies, puppies need to relieve themselves frequently.

Take your puppy out often— every hour for an eight-week-old, for example—and always immediately after sleeping and eating. The older the puppy, the less often he will need to relieve himself. Finally, as a mature healthy adult, he will require only three to five relief trips per day.

HOUSING

Since the types of housing and control you provide for your puppy have a direct relationship on the success of house-training, we consider the various aspects of

CANINE DEVELOPMENT SCHEDULE

It is important to understand how and at what age a puppy develops into adulthood. If you are a puppy owner, consult the following Canine Development Schedule to determine the stage of development your puppy is currently experiencing. This knowledge will help you as you work with the puppy in the weeks and months ahead.

Period	Age	Characteristics
FIRST TO THIRD	BIRTH TO SEVEN WEEKS	Puppy needs food, sleep and warmth, and responds to simple and gentle touching. Needs mother for security and disciplining. Needs littermates for learning and interacting with other dogs. Pup learns to function within a pack and learns pack order of dominance. Begin socializing pup with adults and children for short periods. Pup begins to become aware of his environment.
FOURTH	EIGHT TO TWELVE WEEKS	Brain is fully developed. Needs socializing with outside world. Remove from mother and littermates. Needs to change from canine pack to human pack. Human dominance necessary. Fear period occurs between 8 and 12 weeks. Avoid fright and pain.
FIFTH	THIRTEEN TO SIXTEEN WEEKS	Training and formal obedience should begin. Less association with other dogs, more with people, places, situations. Period will pass easily if you remember this is pup's change-to-adolescence time. Be firm and fair. Flight instinct prominent. Permissiveness and over-disciplining can do permanent damage. Praise for good behavior.
JUVENILE	FOUR TO EIGHT MONTHS	Another fear period about 7 to 8 months of age. It passes quickly, but be cautious of fright and pain. Sexual maturity reached. Dominant traits established. Dog should understand sit, down, come and stay by now.

NOTE: THESE ARE APPROXIMATE TIME FRAMES. ALLOW FOR INDIVIDUAL DIFFERENCES IN PUPPIES.

both before we begin training.

Taking a new puppy home and turning him loose in your house can be compared to turning a child loose in a sports arena and telling the child that the place is all his! The sheer enormity of the place would be too much for him to handle. Instead, offer the puppy clearly defined areas where he can play, sleep, eat and live. A room of the house where the family gathers is the most obvious choice. Puppies are social animals and need to feel a part of the pack right from the start. Hearing your voice, watching you while you are doing things and smelling you nearby are all positive reinforcers that he is now a member of your

THE SUCCESS METHOD

Success that comes by luck is usually short-lived. Success that comes by well-thought-out proven methods is often more easily achieved and permanent. This is the Success Method. It is designed to give you, the puppy owner, a simple yet proven way to help your puppy develop clean living habits and a feeling of security in his new environment.

6 Steps to Successful Crate Training

1 Tell the puppy "Crate time!" and place him in the crate with a small treat (a piece of cheese or half of a biscuit). Let him stay in the crate for five minutes while you are in the same room. Then release him and praise lavishly. Never release him when he is fussing. Wait until he is quiet before you let him out.

2 Repeat Step 1 several times a day.

3 The next day, place the puppy in the crate as before. Let him stay there for ten minutes. Do this several times.

4 Continue building time in five-minute increments until the puppy stays in his crate for 30 minutes with you in the room. Always take him to his relief area after prolonged periods in his crate.

5 Now go back to Step 1 and let the puppy stay in his crate for five minutes, this time while you are out of the room.

6 Once again, build crate time in five-minute increments with you out of the room. When the puppy will stay willingly in his crate (he may even fall asleep!) for 30 minutes with you out of the room, he will be ready to stay in it for several hours at a time.

pack. Usually a family room, the kitchen or a nearby adjoining breakfast area is ideal for providing safety and security for both puppy and owner.

Within the designated room, there should be a smaller area that the puppy can call his own. An alcove, a wire or fiberglass dog crate or a partitioned-off (not boarded!) corner from which he can view the activities of his new family will be fine. The size of the area or crate is the key factor here. The area must be large enough so that the puppy can lie down and stretch out, as well as stand up, without rubbing his head on the top. At the same time, it must be small enough so that he cannot relieve himself at one end and sleep at the other without coming into contact with his droppings. Dogs are, by nature, clean animals and will not remain close to their relief areas unless forced to do so. In those cases, they then become dirty dogs and usually remain that way for life.

The dog's designated area should contain clean bedding and a toy. Do not put food or water in the puppy's crate during house-training, as this will defeat your purpose as well as make the puppy uncomfortable if he always has to "hold it."

CONTROL

By *control*, we mean helping the puppy to create a lifestyle pattern that will be compatible to that of his human pack *(you!)*. Just as we guide little children to learn our way of life, we must show the puppy when it is time to play, eat, sleep, exercise and even entertain himself.

PAPER CAPER

Never line your pup's sleeping area with newspaper. Puppy litters are usually raised on newspaper and, once in your home, the puppy will immediately associate newspaper with voiding. Never put newspaper on any floor while house-training, as this will only confuse the puppy. If you are paper-training him, use paper in his designated relief area only. Finally, restrict water intake after evening meals. Offer a few licks at a time—never let a young puppy gulp water after meals (this goes for adults, too!).

THE CLEAN LIFE

By providing sleeping and resting quarters that fit the dog, and offering frequent opportunities to relieve himself outside his quarters, the puppy quickly learns that the outdoors (or the newspaper if you are training him to paper) is the place to go when he needs to urinate or defecate. It also reinforces his innate desire to keep his sleeping quarters clean. This, in turn, helps develop the muscle control that will eventually produce a dog with clean living habits.

Your puppy should always sleep in his crate. He should also learn that, during times of household confusion and excessive human activity, such as at breakfast when family members are preparing for the day, he can play by himself in relative safety and comfort in his designated area. Each time you leave the puppy alone, he should understand exactly where he is to stay.

Puppies are chewers. They cannot tell the difference between lamp cords, television wires, shoes, table legs, etc. Chewing into a television wire, for example, can be fatal to the puppy, while a shorted wire can start a fire in the house. If the puppy chews on the arm of the chair when he is alone, you will probably discipline him angrily when you get home. Thus, he makes the association that your coming home means he is going to be punished. (He will not remember chewing the chair and is incapable of making the association of the discipline with his naughty deed.) Accustoming the pup to his designated area not only keeps him safe but also avoids his engaging in destructive behaviors when you are not around.

Times of excitement, such as special occasions, family parties, etc., can be fun for the puppy, providing that he can view the activities from the security of his designated area. He is not underfoot and he is not being fed all sorts of tidbits that will probably cause him stomach distress, yet he still feels a part of the fun.

Schedule

A puppy should be taken to his relief area each time he is released from his designated area, after meals, after play sessions and when he first awakens in the morning (at age eight weeks, this can mean 5 a.m.!). The puppy will indicate that he's ready "to go" by circling or sniffing busily—do not misinterpret these signs. For a puppy less than ten weeks of age, a routine of taking him out every hour is necessary. As the puppy grows, he will be able to wait for longer periods of time.

Keep trips to his relief area short. Stay no more than five or six minutes and then return to the house. If he goes during that time, praise him lavishly and take him indoors immediately. If he does not, but he has an accident when you go back indoors, pick him up immediately, say "No! No!" and return to his relief area. Wait a few minutes, then return to the house again. Never hit a puppy or put his face in urine or excrement when he has had an accident!

Once indoors, put the puppy in his crate until you have had time to clean up his accident. Then, release him to the family area and watch him more closely than before. Chances are, his acci-

HOW MANY TIMES A DAY?

AGE	RELIEF TRIPS
To 14 weeks	10
14–22 weeks	8
22–32 weeks	6
Adulthood	4
(dog stops growing)	

These are estimates, of course, but they are a guide to the *minimum* number of opportunities a dog should have each day to relieve himself.

dent was a result of your not picking up his signal or waiting too long before offering him the opportunity to relieve himself. Never hold a grudge against the puppy for accidents.

Let the puppy learn that going outdoors means it is time to relieve himself, not to play. Once trained, he will be able to play indoors and out and still differentiate between the times for play versus the times for relief.

Help him develop regular

hours for naps, being alone, playing by himself and just resting, all in his crate. Encourage him to entertain himself while you are busy with your activities. Let him learn that having you near is comforting, but it is not your main purpose in life to provide him with undivided attention.

Each time you put your puppy in his own area, use the same command, whatever suits best. Soon he will run to his crate or special area when he hears you say those words.

Crate training provides safety for you, the puppy and the home. It also provides the puppy with a feeling of security, and that helps the puppy achieve self-confidence and clean habits. Remember that one of the primary ingredients in house-training your puppy is control. Regardless of your lifestyle, there will always be occasions when you will need to have a place where your dog can stay and be happy and safe. Crate training is the answer for now and in the future.

In conclusion, a few key elements are really all you need for a successful house-training method—consistency, frequency, praise, control and supervision. By following these procedures with a normal, healthy puppy, you and the puppy will soon be past the stage of accidents and ready to move on to a full and rewarding life together.

PLAN TO PLAY
Your dog should also have regular play and exercise sessions when he is with you or a family member. Exercise for a very young puppy can consist of a short walk around the house or yard. Playing can include fetching games with a large ball or a special toy. (All puppies teethe and need soft things upon which to chew.) Remember to restrict play periods to indoors within his living area (the family room, for example) until the dog is completely house-trained.

ROLES OF DISCIPLINE, REWARD AND PUNISHMENT

Discipline, training one to act in accordance with rules, brings order to life. It is as simple as that. Without discipline, particularly in a group society, chaos will reign supreme and the group will eventually perish. Humans and canines are social animals and need some form of discipline in order to function effectively. They must procure food, reproduce to keep their species going and protect their home base and their young. If there were no discipline in the lives of social animals, they would eventually die from starvation and/or predation by other stronger animals.

In the case of domestic canines, discipline in their lives is needed in order for them to understand how their pack (you and other family members) functions and how they must act in order to survive.

A large humane society in a highly populated area recently surveyed dog owners regarding their satisfaction with their relationships with their dogs. People who had trained their dogs were 75% more satisfied with their pets than those who had never trained their dogs.

Dr. Edward Thorndike, a noted psychologist, established *Thorndike's Theory of Learning*, which states that a behavior that results in a pleasant event tends

KEEP SMILING
Never train your dog, puppy or adult, when you are angry or in a sour mood. Dogs are very sensitive to human feelings, especially anger, and if your dog senses that you are angry or upset, he will connect your anger with his training and learn to resent or fear his training sessions.

to be repeated. A behavior that results in an unpleasant event tends not to be repeated. It is this theory upon which training methods are based today. For example, if you manipulate a dog to

A tasty tidbit is all the motivation some puppies need to understand what is expected of them.

perform a specific behavior and reward him for doing it, he is likely to do it again because he enjoyed the end result.

Occasionally, punishment, a penalty inflicted for an offense, is necessary. The best type of punishment often comes from an outside source. For example, a child is told not to touch the stove because he may get burned. He disobeys and touches the stove. In doing so, he receives a burn. From that time on, he respects the heat of the stove and avoids contact with it. Therefore, a behavior that results in an unpleasant event tends not to be repeated.

A good example of a dog learning the hard way is the dog who chases the house cat. He is told many times to leave the cat alone, yet he persists in teasing the cat. Then, one day, the dog begins chasing the cat but the cat turns and swipes a claw across the dog's face, leaving the dog with a painful gash on his nose. The final result is that the dog stops chasing the cat.

TRAINING EQUIPMENT

COLLAR AND LEAD
For a Spanish Water Dog, the collar and leash that you use for training must be one with which you are easily able to work, not too heavy for the dog and perfectly safe.

TREATS
Have a bag of treats on hand; something nutritious and easy to swallow works best. Use a soft treat, a chunk of cheese or a piece of cooked chicken rather than a dry biscuit. By the time the dog has finished chewing a dry treat, he will forget why he is being rewarded in the first place!

Using food rewards will not teach a dog to beg at the table—the only way to teach a dog to beg at the table is to give him food from the table. In training, rewarding the dog with a food treat will help him associate praise and the treats with learning new behaviors that obviously please his owner.

TRAINING BEGINS: ASK THE DOG A QUESTION
In order to teach your dog anything, you must first get his attention. After all, he cannot learn anything if he is looking away from you with his mind on something else.

To get your dog's attention, ask him "School?" and immedi-

COMMAND STANCE

Stand up straight and authoritatively when giving your dog commands. Do not issue commands when lying on the floor or lying on your back on the sofa. If you are on your hands and knees when you give a command, your dog will think you are positioning yourself to play.

that are fun and that result in positive attention for him.

Remember that the dog does not understand your verbal language; he only recognizes sounds. Your question translates to a series of sounds for him, and those sounds become the signal to go to you and pay attention. The dog learns that if he does this, he will get to interact with you plus receive treats and praise.

ately walk over to him and give him a treat as you tell him "Good dog." Wait a minute or two and repeat the routine, this time with a treat in your hand as you approach within a foot of the dog. Do not go directly to him, but stop about a foot short of him and hold out the treat as you ask "School?" He will see you approaching with a treat in your hand and most likely begin walking toward you. As you meet, give him the treat and praise again.

The third time, ask the question, have a treat in your hand and walk only a short distance toward the dog so that he must walk almost all the way to you. As he reaches you, give him the treat and praise again.

By this time, the dog will probably be getting the idea that if he pays attention to you, especially when you ask that question, it will pay off in treats and enjoyable activities for him. In other words, he learns that "school" means doing great things with you

Teaching your Spanish Water Dog the sit command is an excellent place to start his formal education.

The sit-stay command is a natural extension of the sit command. Always end your training session with a successful exercise and lots of praise.

The sit-stay command is a natural extension of the sit command. Always end your training session with a successful exercise and lots of praise.

praise enthusiastically, because dogs relish verbal praise from their owners and feel so proud of themselves whenever they accomplish a behavior.

You will not use food forever in getting the dog to obey your commands. Food is only used to teach new behaviors and, once the dog knows what you want when you give a specific command, you will wean him off the food treats but still maintain the verbal praise. After all, you will always have your voice with you, and there will be many times when you have no food rewards but expect the dog to obey.

THE BASIC COMMANDS

TEACHING SIT

Now that you have the dog's attention, attach his leash and hold it in your left hand, and hold a food treat in your right hand. Place your food hand at the dog's nose and let him lick the treat but not take it from you. Say "Sit" and slowly raise your food hand from in front of the dog's nose up over his head so that he is looking at the ceiling. As he bends his head upward, he will have to bend his knees to maintain his balance. As he bends his knees, he will assume a sit position. At that point, release the food treat and praise lavishly with comments such as "Good dog! Good sit!" Remember to always

TEACHING DOWN

Teaching the down exercise is easy when you understand how the dog perceives the down position, and it is very difficult when you do not. Dogs perceive the down position as a submissive one; therefore, teaching the down exercise by using a forceful method can sometimes make the dog develop such a fear of the down that he either runs away when you say "Down" or he attempts to snap at the person who tries to force him down.

Have the dog sit close alongside your left leg, facing in the same direction as you are. Hold the leash in your left hand and a food treat in your right. Now place your left hand lightly on the top of the dog's shoulders where they meet above the spinal cord. Do not push down on the dog's shoulders; simply rest your left hand there so you can guide the dog to lie down close to your left leg rather than to swing away from your side when he drops.

Now place the food hand at the dog's nose, say "Down" very softly (almost a whisper) and slowly lower the food hand to the dog's front feet. When the food hand reaches the floor, begin moving it forward along the floor in front of the dog. Keep talking softly to the dog, saying things like, "Do you want this treat? You can do this, good dog." Your reassuring tone of voice will help calm the dog as he tries to follow the food hand in order to get the treat.

When the dog's elbows touch the floor, release the food and praise softly. Try to get the dog to maintain that down position for several seconds before you let him sit up again. The goal here is to get the dog to settle down and not feel threatened in the down position.

Teaching Stay

It is easy to teach the dog to stay in either a sit or a down position. Again, we use food and praise during the teaching process as we help the dog to understand exactly what it is that we are expecting him to do.

To teach the sit/stay, start with the dog sitting on your left side as before and hold the leash in your left hand. Have a food treat in your right hand and place your food hand at the dog's nose. Say "Stay" and step out on your right foot to stand directly in front of the dog, toe to toe, as he licks and nibbles the treat. Be sure to keep his head facing upward to maintain the sit position. Count to five and then swing around to stand next to the dog again with him on your

---

DOUBLE JEOPARDY
A dog in jeopardy never lies down. He stays alert on his feet because instinct tells him that he may have to run away or fight for his survival. Therefore, if a dog feels threatened or anxious, he will not lie down. Consequently, it is important to keep the dog calm and relaxed as he learns the down exercise.

left. As soon as you get back to the original position, release the food and praise lavishly.

To teach the down/stay, do the down as previously described. As soon as the dog lies down, say "Stay" and step out on your right foot just as you did in the sit/stay. Count to five and then return to stand beside the dog with him on your left side. Release the treat and praise as always.

Within a week or ten days, you can begin to add a bit of distance between you and your dog when you leave him. When you do, use your left hand open with the palm facing the dog as a stay signal. Hold the food treat in your right hand as before, but this time the food will not be touching the dog's nose. He will watch the food hand and quickly learn that he is going to get that treat as soon as you return to his side.

Too much repetition will make your Spanish Water Dog yawn. Literally!

When you can stand 3 feet away from your dog for 30 seconds, you can then begin building time and distance in both stays. Eventually, the dog can be expected to remain in the stay position for prolonged periods of time until you return to him or call him to you. Always praise lavishly when he stays.

TEACHING COME

If you make teaching "come" an exciting experience, you should never have a student that does not love the game or that fails to come when called. The secret, it seems, is never to teach the word "come."

At times when an owner most wants his dog to come when called, the owner is likely to be upset or anxious and he allows these feelings to come through in the tone of his voice when he calls his dog. Hearing that desperation in his owner's voice, the dog fears the results of going to him and therefore either disobeys outright or runs in the opposite direction. The secret, therefore, is to teach the dog a game and, when you want him to come to you, simply play the game. It is practically a no-fail solution!

To begin, have several members of your family take a few food treats and each go into a different room in the house. Everyone takes turns calling the dog, and each person should celebrate the dog's finding him with a treat and lots of happy praise. When a person calls the dog, he is actually inviting the dog to find him and to get a treat as a reward for winning.

A few turns of the "Where are you?" game and the dog will understand that everyone is playing the game and that each person

has a big celebration awaiting the dog's success at locating him or her. Once the dog learns to love the game, simply calling out "Where are you?" will bring him running from wherever he is when he hears that all-important question.

The come command is recognized as one of the most important things to teach a dog, but there are trainers who work with thousands of dogs and never teach the actual word "come." Yet these dogs will race to respond to a person who uses the dog's name followed by "Where are you?" For example, a woman has a elderly companion dog who went blind, but who never fails to locate her owner when asked, "Where are you?"

Children, in particular, love to play this game with their dogs.

Under that wool lies an intelligent dog with a world of potential for you to develop.

"WHERE ARE YOU?"

When calling the dog, do not say "Come." Say things like, "Rover, where are you? See if you can find me! I have a biscuit for you!" Keep up a constant line of chatter with coaxing sounds and frequent questions such as "Where are you?" The dog will learn to follow the sound of your voice to locate you and receive his reward.

"COME" ... BACK

Never call your dog to come to you for a correction or scold him when he reaches you. That is the quickest way to turn a "Come" command into "Go away fast!" Dogs think only in the present tense, and your dog will connect the scolding with coming to you, not with the misbehavior of a few moments earlier.

Children can hide in smaller places like a shower or bathtub, behind a bed or under a table. The dog needs to work a little bit harder to find these hiding places, but, when he does, he loves to celebrate with a treat and a tussle with a favorite youngster.

TEACHING HEEL

Heeling means that the dog walks beside the owner without pulling. It takes time and patience on the owner's part to succeed at teaching the dog that he (the owner) will not proceed unless the dog is walking calmly beside him. Neither pulling out ahead on the leash nor lagging behind is acceptable.

Begin by holding the leash in your left hand as the dog sits beside your left leg. Move the loop end of the leash to your right hand, but keep your left hand short on the lead so that it keeps the dog in close next to you.

Say "Heel" and step forward on your left foot. Keep the dog close to you and take three steps. Stop and have the dog sit next to you in what we now call the heel position. Praise verbally, but do not touch the dog. Hesitate a moment and begin again with "Heel," taking three steps and stopping, at which point the dog is told to sit again.

Your goal here is to have the dog walk those three steps without pulling on the leash. Once he will walk calmly beside you for three steps without pulling, increase the number of steps you take to five. When he will walk politely beside you while you take five steps, you can increase the length of your walk to ten steps. Keep increasing the length of your stroll until the dog will walk quietly beside you without pulling as long as you want him to heel. When you stop heeling, indicate to the dog that the exer-

convince the dog that you are the leader and that you will be the one to decide on the direction and speed of your travel.

Each time the dog looks up at you or slows down to give a slack leash between the two of you, quietly praise him and say "Good heel. Good dog." Eventually, the dog will begin to respond and within a few days he will be walking politely beside you without pulling on the leash. At first, the training sessions should be kept short and very positive; soon the dog will be able to walk nicely

A dog that will heel politely on leash is a pleasure to walk, whether in a large field or on a busy sidewalk.

cise is over by verbally praising as you pet him and say "OK, good dog." The "OK" is used as a release word, meaning that the exercise is finished and the dog is free to relax.

If you are dealing with a dog who insists on pulling you around, simply "put on your brakes" and stand your ground until the dog realizes that the two of you are not going anywhere until he is beside you and moving at your pace, not his. It may take some time just standing there to

with you for increasingly longer distances. Remember also to give the dog free time and the opportunity to run and play when you have finished heel practice.

WEANING OFF FOOD IN TRAINING

Food is used in training new behaviors. Once the dog understands what behavior goes with a specific command, it is time to start weaning him off the food treats. At first, give a treat after each exercise. Then, start to give a treat only after every other exercise. Mix up the times when you offer a food reward and the times when you only offer praise so that the dog will never know when he is going to receive both food and praise and when he is going to receive only praise. This is called a variable ratio reward system. It proves successful because there is always the chance that the owner will produce a treat, so the dog never stops trying for that reward. No matter what, *always* give verbal praise.

OBEDIENCE CLASSES

It is a good idea to enroll in an obedience class if one is available in your area. If yours is a show dog, handling classes would be more appropriate. Many areas have dog clubs that offer basic obedience training as well as preparatory classes for

---

A BORN PRODIGY

Occasionally, a dog and owner who have not attended formal classes have been able to earn entry-level titles by obtaining competition rules and regulations from a local kennel club and practicing on their own to a degree of perfection. Obtaining the higher level titles, however, almost always requires extensive training under the tutelage of experienced instructors. In addition, the more difficult levels require more specialized equipment whereas the lower levels do not.

---

obedience competition. There are also local dog trainers who offer similar classes.

At obedience trials, dogs can earn titles at various levels of competition. The beginning levels of obedience competition include basic behaviors such as sit, down, heel, etc. The more advanced levels of competition include jumping, retrieving, scent discrimination and signal work. The advanced levels require a dog and owner to put a lot of time and effort into their training. The titles that can be earned at these levels of competition are very prestigious.

OTHER ACTIVITIES FOR LIFE

Whether a dog is trained in the structured environment of a class or alone with his owner at home, there are many activities that can bring fun and rewards to both owner and dog once they have mastered basic control.

Teaching the dog to help out around the home, in the garden or on the farm provides great satisfaction to both dog and owner. In addition, the dog's help makes life a little easier for his owner and raises his stature as a valued companion to his family. It helps give the dog a purpose by occupying his mind and providing an outlet for his energy. With a dog as multi-talented as the Spanish Water Dog, there are a plethora of activities—on land and in the water—that can keep your dog moving toward new goals every weekend.

Backpacking is an exciting and healthy activity that the dog can be taught without assistance from more than his owner. The exercise of walking and climbing is good for man and dog alike, and the bond that they develop together is priceless. The rule for backpacking with any dog is never to expect the dog to carry more than one-sixth of his body weight.

If you are interested in participating in organized competition with your Spanish Water Dog, there are activities other than obedience in which you and your dog can become involved. Agility is a popular sport in which dogs run through an obstacle course that includes various jumps,

tunnels and other exercises to test the dog's speed and coordination. The owners run beside their dogs to give commands and to guide them through the course. Although competitive, the focus is on fun—it's fun to do, fun to watch and great exercise.

Of course, the most exciting sport for Spanish Water Dogs is herding trials, which are sponsored by breed clubs and national kennel clubs. You can also find out about water tests for this diving wonder, which are spectacular events for all breeds of water dogs and retrievers. Some Spanish Water Dogs have been used for search and rescue work, in cases of catastrophes like avalanches, earthquakes and bombings. Tracking events are super ways of training the Spanish Water Dog for such work.

Find out about water dog trials and events in your area. The Spanish Water Dog excels in water sports in which he can apply his superior intelligence and agility.

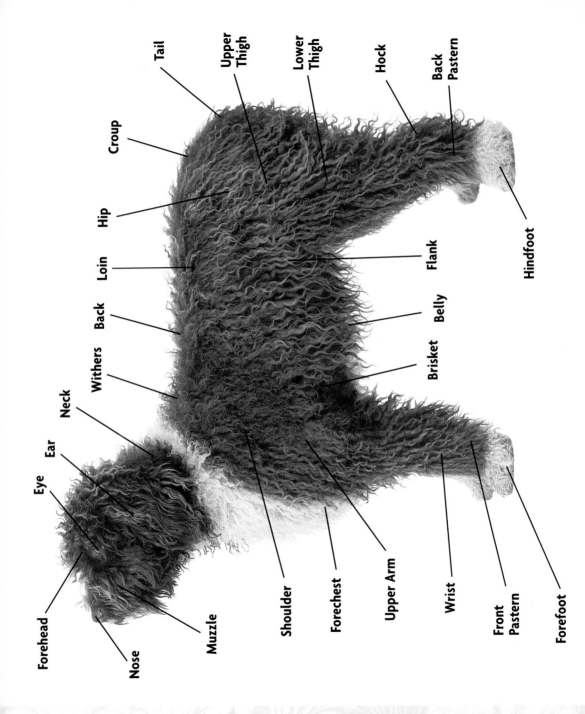

PHYSICAL STRUCTURE OF THE SPANISH WATER DOG

SPANISH WATER DOG

Dogs suffer from many of the same physical illnesses as people and might even share many of the same psychological problems. Since people usually know more about human diseases than canine maladies, many of the terms used in this chapter will be familiar but not necessarily those used by vets. For example, we will use the familiar term *x-ray* instead of *radiograph*. We will also use the familiar term *symptoms*, even though dogs don't have symptoms, which are verbal descriptions of something the patient feels or observes himself that he regards as abnormal. Dogs have *clinical signs* since they cannot speak, so we have to look for these clinical signs…but we still use the term *symptoms* in the book.

Medicine is a constantly changing art, with some scientific input as well. Things alter as we learn more and more about basic sciences such as genetics and biochemistry, and have use of more sophisticated imaging techniques like Computer Aided Tomography (CAT scans) and Magnetic Resonance Imaging (MRI

scans). There is academic dispute about many canine maladies, so different vets treat them in different ways, and some vets have a greater emphasis on surgical techniques than others.

SELECTING A QUALIFIED VET

Your selection of a vet should be based on personal recommendation for his skills with dogs, specifically herding or water breeds if possible. If the vet is based nearby, it will be helpful because you might have an emergency or need to make multiple visits for treatments.

All veterinary professionals are licensed and are capable of handling routine medical issues such as infections, injuries and the promotion of health (for example, by vaccination). If the problem affecting your dog is more complex, your vet will refer your pet to someone with a more detailed knowledge of what is wrong. This will usually be a specialist who concentrates in a specific field, such as veterinary dermatology, veterinary ophthalmology, etc.; whatever is relevant to your dog's problem.

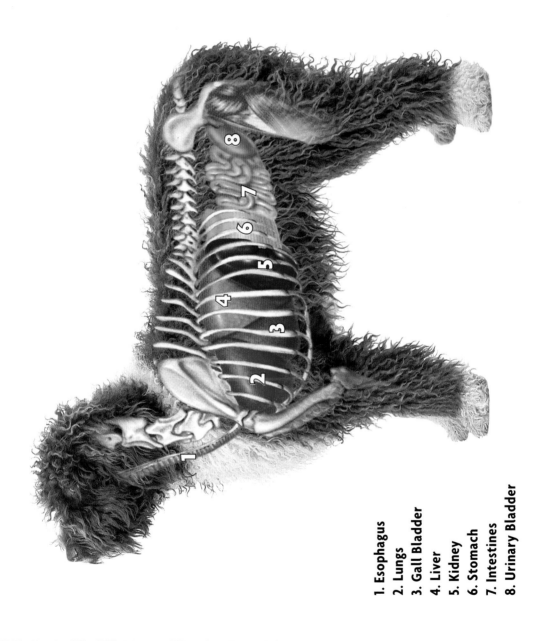

1. Esophagus
2. Lungs
3. Gall Bladder
4. Liver
5. Kidney
6. Stomach
7. Intestines
8. Urinary Bladder

INTERNAL ORGANS OF THE SPANISH WATER DOG

Veterinary procedures are very costly and, as the treatments available improve, they are going to become more expensive. It is quite acceptable to discuss matters of cost with your vet; if there is more than one treatment option, cost may be a factor in deciding which route to take.

PREVENTATIVE MEDICINE

It is much easier, less costly and more effective to practice preventative medicine than to fight bouts of illness and disease. Properly bred puppies of all breeds come from parents that were selected based upon their genetic-disease profiles. The puppies' mother should have been vaccinated, free of all internal and external parasites and properly nourished. For these reasons, a visit to the vet who cared for the dam (mother) is recommended if at all possible. The dam passes disease resistance to her puppies, which should last from eight to ten weeks. Unfortunately, she can also pass on parasites and infection. This is why knowledge about her health is useful in learning more about the health of the puppies.

WEANING TO FIVE MONTHS OLD

Puppies should be weaned by the time they are two months old. A puppy that remains for at least eight weeks with his mother and littermates usually adapts better to other dogs and people later in his life.

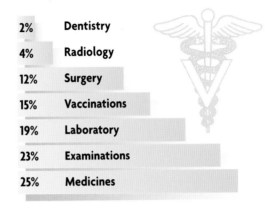

Breakdown of Veterinary Income by Category

2%	Dentistry
4%	Radiology
12%	Surgery
15%	Vaccinations
19%	Laboratory
23%	Examinations
25%	Medicines

A typical vet's income, categorized according to services performed. This survey dealt with small-animal (pets) practices.

Sometimes new owners have their puppy examined by a vet immediately, which is a good idea unless the puppy is over-tired by a long journey, in which case an appointment should be made for the next day or so.

The puppy will have his teeth examined and his skeletal conformation and general health checked prior to certification by the vet. Puppies in certain breeds have problems with their kneecaps, cataracts and other eye problems, heart murmurs and undescended testicles. Your vet might also have training in temperament testing. At the first visit, the vet will set up a schedule for your pup's vaccinations.

VACCINATION SCHEDULING

Most vaccinations are given by injection and should only be

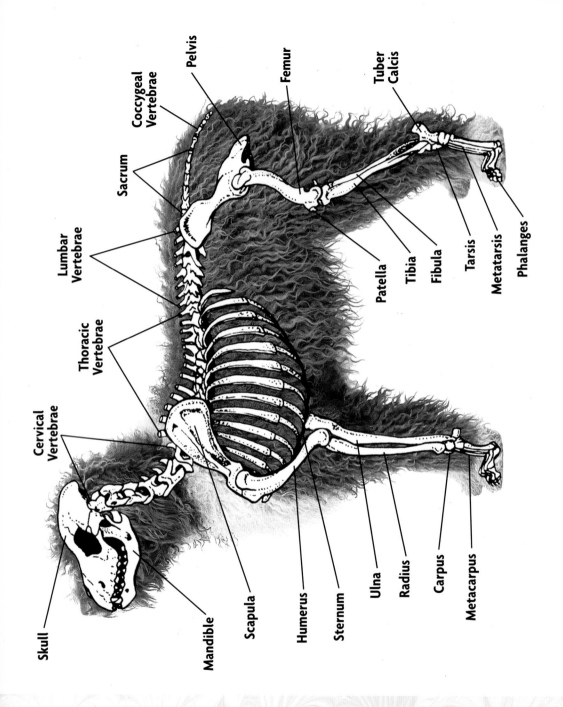

Coccygeal Vertebrae
Pelvis
Femur
Tuber Calcis
Sacrum
Lumbar Vertebrae
Thoracic Vertebrae
Cervical Vertebrae
Patella
Tibia
Fibula
Tarsis
Metatarsis
Phalanges
Skull
Mandible
Scapula
Humerus
Sternum
Ulna
Radius
Carpus
Metacarpus

SKELETAL STRUCTURE OF THE SPANISH WATER DOG

given by a vet. Both he and you should keep a record of the date of the injection, the identification of the vaccine and the amount given. Some vets give a first vaccination at eight weeks, but most dog breeders prefer the course not to commence until about ten weeks because of the risk of interaction with the antibodies produced by the mother. The vaccination scheduling is usually based on a 15-day cycle. You must take your vet's advice as to when to vaccinate, as this may differ according to the vaccine used.

The usual vaccines contain immunizing doses of several different viruses such as distemper, parvovirus, parainfluenza and hepatitis. There are other vaccines available when the puppy is at risk. You should rely upon professional advice. This is especially true for the booster immunizations. Most vaccination programs require a booster when the puppy is a year old and once a year thereafter. In some cases, circumstances may require more or less frequent immunizations.

Kennel cough, more formally known as tracheobronchitis, is immunized against with a vaccine that is sprayed into the dog's nostrils. Kennel cough is usually

HEALTH AND VACCINATION SCHEDULE

Age in Weeks:	6th	8th	10th	12th	14th	16th	20-24th	52nd
Worm Control	✔	✔	✔	✔	✔	✔	✔	
Neutering								✔
Heartworm		✔		✔		✔	✔	
Parvovirus	✔		✔		✔		✔	✔
Distemper		✔		✔		✔		✔
Hepatitis		✔		✔		✔		✔
Leptospirosis								✔
Parainfluenza	✔		✔		✔			✔
Dental Examination		✔					✔	✔
Complete Physical		✔					✔	✔
Coronavirus				✔			✔	✔
Kennel Cough	✔							
Hip Dysplasia								✔
Rabies							✔	

Vaccinations are not instantly effective. It takes about two weeks for the dog's immune system to develop antibodies. Most vaccinations require annual booster shots. Your vet should guide you in this regard.

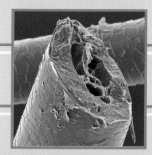

Normal hairs of a dog enlarged 200 times original size. The cuticle (outer covering) is clean and healthy. Unlike human hair that grows from the base, a dog's hair also grows from the end. Damaged hairs and split ends, illustrated above.

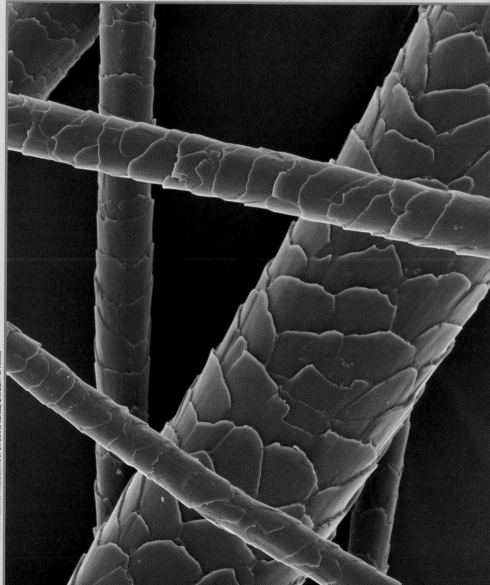

DISEASE REFERENCE CHART

	What is it?	What causes it?	Symptoms
Leptospirosis	Severe disease that affects the internal organs; can be spread to people.	A bacterium, which is often carried by rodents, that enters through mucous membranes and spreads quickly throughout the body.	Range from fever, vomiting and loss of appetite in less severe cases to shock, irreversible kidney damage and possibly death in most severe cases.
Rabies	Potentially deadly virus that infects warm-blooded mammals.	Bite from a carrier of the virus, mainly wild animals.	1st stage: dog exhibits change in behavior, fear. 2nd stage: dog's behavior becomes more aggressive. 3rd stage: loss of coordination, trouble with bodily functions.
Parvovirus	Highly contagious virus, potentially deadly.	Ingestion of the virus, which is usually spread through the feces of infected dogs.	Most common: severe diarrhea. Also vomiting, fatigue, lack of appetite.
Kennel cough	Contagious respiratory infection.	Combination of types of bacteria and virus. Most common: *Bordetella bronchiseptica* bacteria and parainfluenza virus.	Chronic cough.
Distemper	Disease primarily affecting respiratory and nervous system.	Virus that is related to the human measles virus.	Mild symptoms such as fever, lack of appetite and mucus secretion progress to evidence of brain damage, "hard pad."
Hepatitis	Virus primarily affecting the liver.	Canine adenovirus type I (CAV-1). Enters system when dog breathes in particles.	Lesser symptoms include listlessness, diarrhea, vomiting. More severe symptoms include "blue-eye" (clumps of virus in eye).
Coronavirus	Virus resulting in digestive problems.	Virus is spread through infected dog's feces.	Stomach upset evidenced by lack of appetite, vomiting, diarrhea.

included in routine vaccination, but it is often not as effective as the vaccines for other major diseases.

FIVE MONTHS TO ONE YEAR OF AGE
Unless you intend to breed or show your dog, neutering the puppy around six months of age is recommended. Neutering/ spaying has proven to be extremely beneficial to male and female dogs, respectively. Besides eliminating the possibility of pregnancy, it inhibits (but does not prevent) breast cancer in bitches and prostate cancer in male dogs.

Discuss all aspects of the procedure with your vet. Sometimes opinions vary on the best age to have this done.

Your vet should provide your puppy with a thorough dental evaluation at six months of age, ascertaining whether all of the permanent teeth have erupted properly. A home dental-care regimen should be initiated at six months, including brushing weekly and providing good dental devices (such as nylon bones). Regular dental care promotes healthy teeth, fresh breath and a longer life.

DOGS OLDER THAN ONE YEAR

Continue to visit the vet at least once a year. There is no such disease as "old age," but bodily functions do change with age. The eyes and ears are no longer as efficient. Liver, kidney and intestinal functions often decline. Proper dietary changes, recommended by your vet, can make life more pleasant for your aging Spanish Water Dog and you.

SKIN PROBLEMS

Vets are consulted by dog owners for skin problems more than for any other group of diseases or maladies. A dog's skin is as sensitive, if not more so, than human skin, and both suffer from almost the same ailments (though the occurrence of acne in most dogs is rare!). For this reason, veterinary dermatology has developed into a specialty practiced by many veterinary professionals.

Since many skin problems have visual symptoms that are almost identical, it requires the skill of an experienced veterinary dermatologist to identify and cure many of the more severe skin disorders. Pet shops sell many treatments for skin problems, but most of the treatments are directed at symptoms and not at the underlying problem(s). If your dog is suffering from a skin disorder, you should seek professional assistance as quickly as possible. As with all diseases, the earlier a problem is identified and treated, the better the chances are that the cure will be successful.

HEREDITARY SKIN DISORDERS

Veterinary dermatologists are currently researching a number of skin disorders that are believed to have a hereditary basis. These inherited diseases are transmitted by both parents, who appear (phenotypically) normal but have a recessive gene for the disease, meaning that they carry, but are not affected by, the disease. These diseases pose serious problems to breeders because in some instances there are no methods of identifying carriers. Often the secondary diseases associated with these skin conditions are even more debilitating than the skin disorders themselves, including cancers and respiratory problems.

Among the hereditary skin disorders, for which the mode of inheritance is known, are acrodermatitis, cutaneous asthenia (Ehlers-Danlos syndrome), sebaceous adenitis, cyclic hematopoiesis, dermatomyositis, IgA deficiency, color dilution alopecia and nodular dermatofibrosis. Some of these disorders are limited to one or two breeds, while others affect a large number of breeds. All inherited diseases must be diagnosed and treated by a veterinary specialist.

PARASITE BITES

Many of us are allergic to insect bites. The bites itch, erupt and may even become infected. Dogs have the same reaction to fleas, ticks and/or mites. When an insect lands on you, you have the chance to whisk it away with your hand. Unfortunately, when a dog is bitten by a flea, tick or mite, it can only scratch it away or bite it. By the time the dog has been bitten, the parasite has done some of its damage. It may also have laid eggs, which will cause further problems in the near future. The itching from parasite bites is probably due to the saliva injected into the site when the parasite sucks the dog's blood.

AIRBORNE ALLERGIES

Just as humans suffer from hay fever during the pollinating season, many dogs suffer from the same allergies. When the pollen count is high, your dog might suffer but don't expect him to sneeze and a have a runny nose as a human would. Dogs react to pollen allergies in the same way they react to fleas—they scratch and bite themselves. Dogs, like humans, can be tested for allergens. Discuss the testing with your vet.

AUTO-IMMUNE ILLNESSES

An auto-immune illness is one in which the immune system over-acts and does not recognize parts

THE SAME ALLERGIES
Chances are that you and your dog will have the same allergies. Your allergies are readily recognizable and usually easily treated. Your dog's allergies may be masked.

of the affected person; rather, the immune system starts to react as if these parts were foreign and need to be destroyed. An example is rheumatoid arthritis, which occurs when the body does not recognize the joints, thus leading to a very painful and damaging reaction in the joints. This has nothing to do with age, so can

DENTAL HEALTH

A dental examination is in order when the dog is between six months and one of age so that any permanent teeth that have erupted incorrectly can be corrected. It is important to begin a brushing routine, at home, using dental-care products made for dogs such as toothbrushes and canine toothpaste. Durable nylon and safe edible chews should be a part of your dog's arsenal for good health, good teeth and pleasant breath. The vast majority of dogs three to four years old and older has diseases of the gums from lack of dental attention. Using the various types of dental chews can be very effective in controlling dental plaque.

occur in children. The wear-and-tear arthritis of the older person or dog is osteoarthritis.

Lupus is an auto-immune disease that affects dogs as well as people. It can take variable forms, affecting the kidneys, bones and skin. It can be fatal, so is treated with steroids, which can themselves have very significant side effects. The steroids calm down the allergic reaction to the body's tissues, which helps the lupus, but they also decrease the body's reaction to real foreign substances such as bacteria, and also thins the skin and bones.

FOOD PROBLEMS

FOOD ALLERGIES

Dogs are allergic to many foods that may be best-sellers and highly recommended by breeders and vets. Changing the brand of food that you buy may not eliminate the problem if the element to which the dog is allergic is contained in the new brand.

Recognizing a food allergy can be difficult. Humans often have rashes when they eat foods to which they are allergic, or have swelling of the lips or eyes. Dogs do not usually develop rashes, but react in the same way as they do to an airborne or bite allergy—they itch, scratch and bite. While pollen allergies and parasite bites are usually seasonal, pollen allergies are year-round problems.

TREATING FOOD ALLERGY

Diagnosis of food allergy is based on a two- to four-week dietary trial with a home-cooked diet fed to the exclusion of all other foods. The diet should consist of boiled rice or potato with a source of protein that the dog has never eaten before, such as fresh or frozen fish, lamb or even something as exotic as pheasant. Water has to be the only drink, and it is really important that no other foods are fed during this trial. If the dog's condition improves, you will need to try the original diet once again to see if the itching resumes. If it does, then this confirms the diagnosis that the dog is allergic to his original diet. The treatment is long-term feeding of something that does not distress the dog's skin, which may be in the form of one of the commercially available hypoallergenic diets or the home-made diet that you created for the allergy trial.

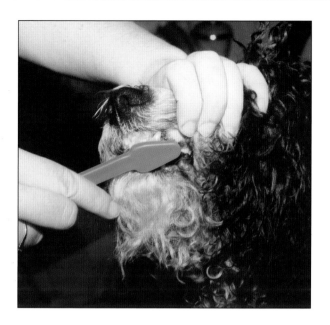

SKIN PROBLEMS

Eczema and dermatitis are skin problems that occur in many breeds, and they can often be tricky problems to solve. Frequently bathing the dog will remove skin oils and will cause the problem to worsen. Allergies to food or to something in the environment can also cause the problem. Consider trying homeopathic remedies in addition to seeing your vet for direction.

FOOD INTOLERANCE

Food intolerance is the inability of the dog to completely digest certain foods. This occurs because the dog does not have the chemicals necessary to digest some foodstuffs. These chemicals are called enzymes. All puppies have the enzymes necessary to digest canine milk, but some dogs do not have the enzymes to digest a very different form of milk that is commonly found in human households—milk from cows. In such dogs, drinking cows' milk results in loose bowels, stomach pains and the passage of gas.

Dogs often do not have the enzymes to digest soy or other beans. The treatment is to exclude the foodstuffs that upset your Spanish Water Dog's digestion.

Don't neglect your dog's teeth. Brush your Spanish Water Dog's teeth about once a week. Use a toothpaste and brush designed especially for dogs.

A male dog flea, *Ctenocephalides canis.*

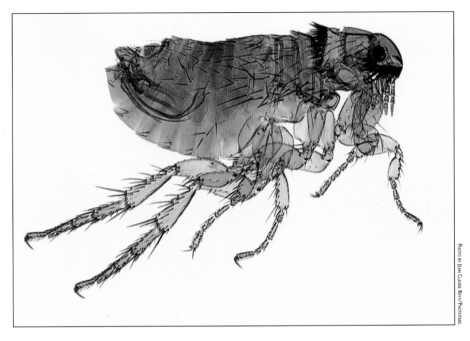

PHOTO BY JEAN CLAUDE REVY/PHOTOTAKE.

EXTERNAL PARASITES

FLEAS

Of all the problems to which dogs are prone, none is more well known and frustrating than fleas. Flea infestation is relatively simple to cure but difficult to prevent. Parasites that are harbored inside the body are a bit more difficult to eradicate but they are easier to control.

To control flea infestation, you have to understand the flea's life cycle. Fleas are often thought of as a summertime problem, but centrally heated homes have changed the patterns and fleas can be found at any time of the year. The most effective method of flea control is a two-stage approach: one stage to kill the adult fleas, and the other to control the development of pre-adult fleas. Unfortunately, no single active ingredient is effective against all stages of the life cycle.

FLEA KILLER CAUTION— "POISON"

Flea-killers are poisonous. You should not spray these toxic chemicals on areas of a dog's body that he licks, including his genitals and his face. Flea killers taken internally are a better answer, but check with your vet in case internal therapy is not advised for your dog.

LIFE CYCLE STAGES

During its life, a flea will pass through four life stages: egg, larva, pupa or nymph and adult. The adult stage is the most visible and irritating stage of the flea life cycle, and this is why the majority of flea-control products concentrate on this stage. The fact is that adult fleas account for only 1% of the total flea population, and the other 99% exist in pre-adult stages, i.e., eggs, larvae and nymphs. The pre-adult stages are barely visible to the naked eye.

THE LIFE CYCLE OF THE FLEA

Eggs are laid on the dog, usually in quantities of about 20 or 30, several times a day. The adult female flea must have a blood meal before each egg-laying session. When first laid, the eggs will cling to the dog's hair, as the eggs are still moist. However, they will quickly dry out and fall from the dog, especially if the dog moves around or scratches. Many eggs will fall off in the dog's favorite area or an area in which he spends a lot of time, such as his bed.

Once the eggs fall from the dog onto the carpet or furniture, they will hatch into larvae. This takes from one to ten days. Larvae are not particularly mobile and will usually travel only a few inches from where they hatch. However, they do have a tendency to move away from bright light and heavy

> ### EN GARDE:
> ### CATCHING FLEAS OFF GUARD!
> Consider the following ways to arm yourself against fleas:
> - Add a small amount of pennyroyal or eucalyptus oil to your dog's bath. These natural remedies repel fleas.
> - Supplement your dog's food with fresh garlic (minced or grated) and a hearty amount of brewer's yeast, both of which ward off fleas.
> - Use a flea comb on your dog daily. Submerge fleas in a cup of bleach to kill them quickly.
> - Confine the dog to only a few rooms to limit the spread of fleas in the home.
> - Vacuum daily...and get all of the crevices! Dispose of the bag every few days until the problem is under control.
> - Wash your dog's bedding daily. Cover cushions where your dog sleeps with towels, and wash the towels often.

traffic—under furniture and behind doors are common places to find high quantities of flea larvae.

The flea larvae feed on dead organic matter, including adult flea feces, until they are ready to change into adult fleas. Fleas will usually remain as larvae for around seven days. After this period, the larvae will pupate into protective pupae. While inside the pupae, the larvae will undergo

Fleas have been measured as being able to jump 300,000 times and can jump 150 times their length in any direction, including straight up.

metamorphosis and change into adult fleas. This can take as little time as a few days, but the adult fleas can remain inside the pupae waiting to hatch for up to two years. The pupae are signaled to hatch by certain stimuli, such as physical pressure—the pupae's being stepped on, heat from an animal's lying on the pupae or increased carbon-dioxide levels and vibrations—indicating that a suitable host is available.

Once hatched, the adult flea must feed within a few days. Once the adult flea finds a host, it will not leave voluntarily. It only becomes dislodged by grooming or the host animal's scratching.

PHOTO BY DWIGHT R. KUHL.

The adult flea will remain on the host for the duration of its life unless forcibly removed.

TREATING THE ENVIRONMENT AND THE DOG

Treating fleas should be a two-pronged attack. First, the environment needs to be treated; this includes carpets and furniture, especially the dog's bedding and areas underneath furniture. The environment should be treated with a household spray containing an Insect Growth Regulator (IGR) and an insecticide to kill the adult fleas. Most IGRs are effective against eggs and larvae; they actually mimic the fleas' own hormones and stop the eggs and larvae from developing into adult fleas. There are currently no treatments available to attack the pupa stage of the life cycle, so the adult insecticide is used to kill the newly hatched adult fleas before they find a host. Most IGRs are active for many months, while

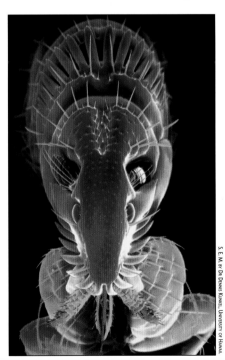

A scanning electron micrograph of a dog or cat flea, *Ctenocephalides*, magnified more than 100x. This image has been colorized for effect.

S. E. M. BY DR DENNIS KUNKEL, UNIVERSITY OF HAWAII.

THE LIFE CYCLE OF THE FLEA

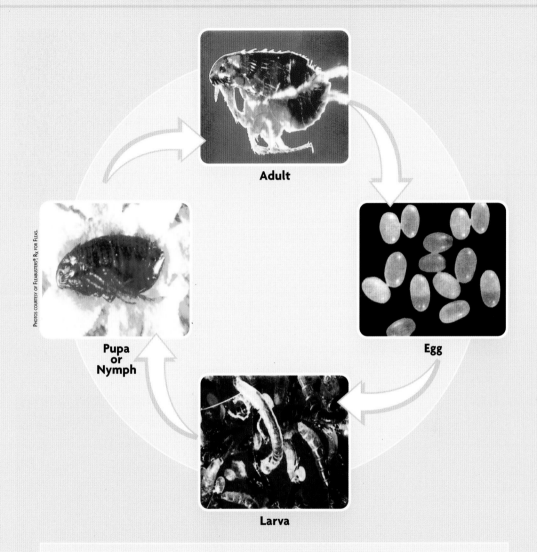

Adult

Egg

Larva

Pupa
or
Nymph

Fleas have been around for millions of years and have adapted to changing host animals. They are able to go through a complete life cycle in less than one month or they can extend their lives to almost two years by remaining as pupae or cocoons. They do not need blood or any other food for up to 20 months.

The second stage of treatment is to apply an adult insecticide to the dog. Traditionally, this would be in the form of a collar or a spray, but more recent innovations include digestible insecticides that poison the fleas when they ingest the dog's blood. Alternatively, there are drops that, when placed on the back of the dog's neck, spread throughout the hair and skin to kill adult fleas.

TICKS

Though not as common as fleas, ticks are found all over the tropical and temperate world. They don't bite, like fleas; they harpoon. They dig their sharp proboscis (nose) into the dog's skin and drink the blood. Their

The American dog tick, Dermacentor variabilis, is probably the most common tick found on dogs. Look at the strength in its eight legs! No wonder it's hard to detach them.

adult insecticides are only active for a few days.

When treating with a house-hold spray, it is a good idea to vacuum before applying the product. This stimulates as many pupae as possible to hatch into adult fleas. The vacuum cleaner should also be treated with an insecticide to prevent the eggs and larvae that have been collected in the vacuum bag from hatching.

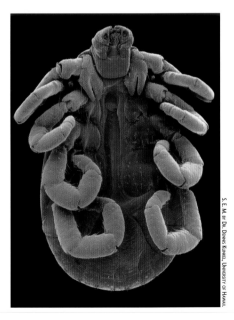

only food and drink is dog's blood. Dogs can get Lyme disease, Rocky Mountain spotted fever, tick bite paralysis and many other diseases from ticks. They may live where fleas are found and they like to hide in cracks or seams in walls. They are controlled the same way fleas are controlled.

The American dog tick, *Dermacentor variabilis*, may well be the most common dog tick in many geographical areas, especially those areas where the climate is hot and humid. Most dog ticks have life expectancies of a week to six months, depending upon climatic conditions. They can neither jump nor fly, but they can crawl slowly and can range up to 16 feet to reach a sleeping or unsuspecting dog.

MITES

Just as fleas and ticks can be problematic for your dog, mites can also lead to an itchy nuisance. Microscopic in size, mites are related to ticks and generally take up permanent residence on their host animal—in this case, your dog! The term *mange* refers to any infestation caused by one of the mighty mites, of which there are six varieties that concern dog owners.

Demodex mites cause a condition known as demodicosis

DEER-TICK CROSSING
The great outdoors may be fun for your dog, but it also is an home to dangerous ticks. Deer ticks carry a bacterium known as *Borrelia burgdorferi* and are most active in the autumn and spring. When infections are caught early, penicillin and tetracycline are effective antibiotics, but, if left untreated, the bacteria may cause neurological, kidney and cardiac problems as well as long-term trouble with walking and painful joints.

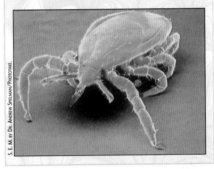

S. E. M. BY DR. ANDREW SPIELMAN/PHOTOTAKE.

PHOTO BY DR. DENNIS KUNKEL, UNIVERSITY OF HAWAII.

The head of an American dog tick, *Dermacentor variabilis*, enlarged and colorized for effect.

The mange mite, *Psoroptes bovis,* can infest cattle and other domestic animals.

PHOTO BY JAMES HAYDEN/YOAV/PHOTOTAKE.

(sometimes called red mange or follicular mange), in which the mites live in the dog's hair follicles and sebaceous glands in larger-than-normal numbers. This type of mange is commonly passed from the dam to her puppies and usually shows up on the puppies' muzzles, though demodicosis is not transferable from one normal dog to another. Most dogs recover from this type of mange without any treatment, though topical therapies are commonly prescribed by the vet.

Human lice look like dog lice; the two are closely related.

PHOTO BY DWIGHT R. KUHN.

The *Cheyletiellosis* mite is the hook-mouthed culprit associated with "walking dandruff," a condition that affects dogs as well as cats and rabbits. This mite lives on the surface of the animal's skin and is readily transferable through direct or indirect contact with an affected animal. The dandruff is present in the form of scaly skin, which may or may not be itchy. If not treated, this mange can affect a whole kennel of dogs and can be spread to humans as well.

The *Sarcoptes* mite causes intense itching on the dog in the form of a condition known as scabies or sarcoptic mange. The cycle of the *Sarcoptes* mite lasts about three weeks, and the mites live in the top layer of the dog's skin (epidermis), preferably in areas with little hair. Scabies is highly contagious and can be passed to humans. Sometimes an allergic reaction to the mite worsens the severe itching associated with sarcoptic mange.

Ear mites, *Otodectes cynotis,* lead to otodectic mange, which most commonly affects the outer ear canal of the dog, though other areas can be affected as well. Dogs with ear-mite infestation commonly scratch at their ears, causing further irritation, and shake their heads. Dark brown droppings in the outer ear confirm the diagnosis. Your vet can prescribe a treatment to flush out the ears and kill any eggs in the ears. A complete month of treatment is necessary to cure the mange.

Two other mites, less common in dogs, include *Dermanyssus gallinae* (the poultry or red mite) and *Eutrombicula alfreddugesi* (the North American mite associated with trombiculidiasis or chigger infestation). The poultry mite frequently lives on chickens, but can transfer to dogs who spend time near farm animals. Chigger infestation affects dogs in the

---

NOT A DROP TO DRINK
Never allow your dog to swim in polluted water or public areas where water quality can be suspect. Even perfectly clear water can harbor parasites, many of which can cause serious to fatal illnesses in canines. Areas inhabited by water-fowl and other wildlife are especially dangerous.

Central US who have exposure to woodlands. The types of mange caused by both of these mites are treatable by vets.

INTERNAL PARASITES

Most animals—fishes, birds and mammals, including dogs and humans—have worms and other parasites that live inside their bodies. According to Dr. Herbert R. Axelrod, the fish pathologist, there are two kinds of parasites: dumb and smart. The smart parasites live in peaceful cooperation with their hosts (symbiosis), while the dumb parasites kill their hosts. Most worm infections are relatively easy to control. If they are not controlled, they weaken the host dog to the point that other medical problems occur, but they do not kill the host as dumb parasites would.

A brown dog tick, *Rhipicephalus sanguineus*, is an uncommon but annoying tick found on dogs.
PHOTO BY CAROLINA BIOLOGICAL SUPPLY/PHOTOTAKE.

DO NOT MIX
Never mix parasite-control products without first consulting your vet. Some products can become toxic when combined with others and can cause fatal consequences.

The roundworm *Rhabditis* can infect both dogs and humans.

ROUNDWORMS

Average-size dogs can pass 1,360,000 roundworm eggs every day. For example, if there were only 1 million dogs in the world, the world would be saturated with thousands of tons of dog feces. These feces would contain around 15,000,000,000 roundworm eggs.

Up to 31% of home yards and children's sand boxes in the US contain roundworm eggs.

Flushing dog's feces down the toilet is not a safe practice because the usual sewage treatments do not destroy roundworm eggs.

Infected puppies start shedding roundworm eggs at three weeks of age. They can be infected by their mother's milk.

The roundworm, *Ascaris lumbricoides.*

ROUNDWORMS

The roundworms that infect dogs are known scientifically as *Toxocara canis*. They live in the dog's intestines and shed eggs continually. It has been estimated that a dog produces about 6 or more ounces of feces every day. Each ounce of feces averages hundreds of thousands of roundworm eggs. There are no known areas in which dogs roam that do not contain roundworm eggs. The greatest danger of roundworms is that they infect people, too! It is wise to have your dog tested regularly for round-worms.

In young puppies, round-worms cause bloated bellies, diarrhea, coughing and vomiting, and are transmitted from the dam (through blood or milk). Affected puppies will not appear as animated as normal puppies. The worms appear spaghetti-like, measuring as long as 6 inches. Adult dogs can acquire round-worms through coprophagia (eating contaminated feces) or by killing rodents that carry round-worms.

Roundworm infection can kill puppies and cause severe problems in adults, as the hatched larvae travel to the lungs and trachea through the bloodstream. Cleanliness is the best preventative for roundworms. Always pick up after your dog and dispose of feces in appropriate receptacles.

The hookworm, *Ancylostoma caninum.*

HOOKWORMS

In the United States, dog owners have to be concerned about four different species of hookworm, the most common and most serious of which is *Ancylostoma caninum,* which prefers warm climates. The others are *Ancylostoma braziliense, Ancylostoma tubaeforme* and *Uncinaria stenocephala,* the latter of which is a concern to dogs living in the Northern US and Canada, as this species prefers cold climates. Hookworms are dangerous to humans as well as to dogs and cats, and can be the cause of severe anemia due to iron deficiency. The worm uses its teeth to attach itself to the dog's intestines and changes the site of its attachment about six times per day. Each time the worm repositions itself, the dog loses

blood and can become anemic. *Ancylostoma caninum* is the most likely of the four species to cause anemia in the dog.

Symptoms of hookworm infection include dark stools, weight loss, general weakness, pale coloration and anemia, as well as possible skin problems. Fortunately, hookworms are easily purged from the affected dog with a number of medications that have proven effective. Discuss these with your vet. Most heartworm preventatives include a hookworm insecticide as well.

Owners also must be aware that hookworms can infect humans, who can acquire the larvae through exposure to contaminated feces. Since the worms cannot complete their life cycle on a human, the worms simply infest the skin and cause irritation. This condition is known as cutaneous larva migrans syndrome. As a preventative, use disposable gloves or a "poop-scoop" to pick up your dog's droppings and prevent your dog (or neighborhood cats) from defecating in children's play areas.

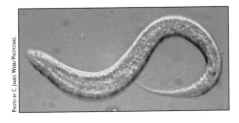

The infective stage of the hookworm larva.

TAPEWORMS

Humans, rats, squirrels, foxes, coyotes, wolves and domestic dogs are all susceptible to tapeworm infection. Except in humans, tapeworms are usually not a fatal infection. Infected individuals can harbor 1000 parasitic worms.

Tapeworms, like some other types of worm, are hermaphroditic, meaning male and female in the same worm.

If dogs eat infected rats or mice, or anything else infected with tapeworm, they get the tapeworm disease. One month after attaching to a dog's intestine, the worm starts shedding eggs. These eggs are infective immediately. Infective eggs can live for a few months without a host animal.

The head and rostellum (the round prominence on the scolex) of a tapeworm, which infects dogs and humans.

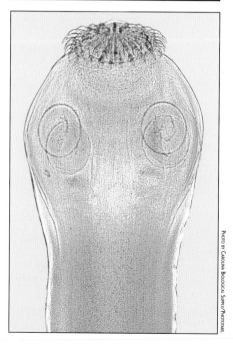

PHOTO BY CAROLINA BIOLOGICAL SUPPLY/PHOTOTAKE

TAPEWORMS

There are many species of tapeworm, all of which are carried by fleas! The most common tapeworm affecting dogs is known as *Dipylidium caninum*. The dog eats the flea and starts the tapeworm cycle. Humans can also be infected with tapeworms—so don't eat fleas! Fleas are so small that your dog could pass them onto your hands, your plate or your food and thus make it possible for you to ingest a flea that is carrying tapeworm eggs.

While tapeworm infection is not life-threatening in dogs (smart parasite!), it can be the cause of a very serious liver disease for humans. About 50% of the humans infected with *Echinococcus multilocularis*, a type of tapeworm that causes alveolar hydatid, perish.

WHIPWORMS

In North America, whipworms are counted among the most common parasitic worms in dogs. The whipworm's scientific name is *Trichuris vulpis*. These worms attach themselves in the lower parts of the intestine, where they feed. Affected dogs may only experience upset tummies, colic and diarrhea. These worms, however, can live for months or years in the dog, beginning their larval stage in the small intestine, spending their adult stage in the large intestine and finally passing infective eggs through the dog's feces. The only way to detect whipworms is through a fecal examination, though this is not always foolproof. Treatment for whipworms is tricky, due to the worms' unusual life-cycle pattern, and very often dogs are reinfected due to exposure to infective eggs on the ground. The whipworm eggs can survive in the environment for as long as five years, thus cleaning up droppings in your own backyard as well as in public places is absolutely essential for sanitation purposes and the health of your dog and others.

THREADWORMS
Though less common than round-worms, hookworms and those previously mentioned, thread-worms concern dog owners in the Southwestern US and Gulf Coast area where the climate is hot and humid. Living in the small intestine of the dog, this worm measures a mere 2 millimeters and is round in shape. Like that of the whipworm, the threadworm's life cycle is very complex and the eggs and larvae are passed through the feces. A deadly disease in humans, *Strongyloides* readily infects people, and the handling of feces is the most common means of transmission. Threadworms are most often seen in young puppies; bloody diarrhea and pneumonia are symptoms. Sick puppies must be isolated and treated immediately; vets recommend a follow-up treatment one month later.

HEARTWORM PREVENTATIVES

There are many heartworm preventatives on the market, many of which are sold at your veterinarian's office. These products can be given daily or monthly, depending on the manufacturer's instructions. All of these preventatives contain chemical insecticides directed at killing heartworms, which leads to some controversy among dog owners. In effect, heartworm preventatives are necessary evils, though you should determine how necessary based on your pet's lifestyle. There is no doubt that heartworm is a dreadful disease that threatens the life of dogs. However, the likelihood of your dog's being bitten by an infected mosquito is slim in most places, and a mosquito-repellent (or an herbal remedy such as Wormwood or Black Walnut) is much safer for your dog and will not compromise his immune system (the way heartworm preventatives will). Should you decide to use the traditional preventative "medications," you can consider giving the pill every other or third month. Since the toxins in the pill will kill the heartworms at all stages of development, the pill would be effective in killing larvae, nymphs or adults and it takes four months for the larvae to reach the adult stage. Thus, there is no rationale to poisoning the dog's system on a monthly basis. Lastly, do not give the pill during the winter months since there are no mosquitoes around to pass on their infection, unless you live in a tropical environment.

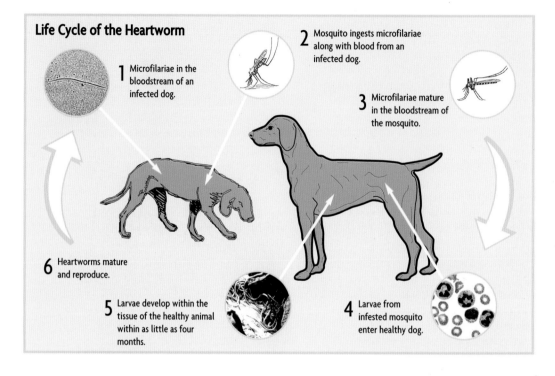

Life Cycle of the Heartworm

1 Microfilariae in the bloodstream of an infected dog.

2 Mosquito ingests microfilariae along with blood from an infected dog.

3 Microfilariae mature in the bloodstream of the mosquito.

6 Heartworms mature and reproduce.

5 Larvae develop within the tissue of the healthy animal within as little as four months.

4 Larvae from infested mosquito enter healthy dog.

HEARTWORMS

Heartworms are thin, extended worms up to 12 inches long, which live in a dog's heart and the major blood vessels surrounding it. Dogs may have up to 200 worms. Symptoms may be loss of energy, loss of appetite, coughing, the development of a pot belly and anemia.

Heartworms are transmitted by mosquitoes. The mosquito drinks the blood of an infected dog and takes in larvae with the blood. The larvae, called microfilariae, develop within the body of the mosquito and are passed on to the next dog bitten after the larvae mature. It takes two to three weeks for the larvae to develop to the infective stage within the body of the mosquito. Dogs are usually treated at about six weeks of age and maintained on a prophylactic dose given monthly.

Blood testing for heartworms is not necessarily indicative of how seriously your dog is infected. Although this is a dangerous disease, it is not easy for a dog to be infected. Discuss the various preventatives with your vet, as there are many different types now available. Together you can decide on a safe course of prevention for your dog.

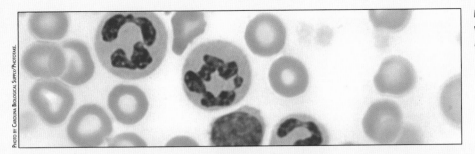

Magnified heart-worm larvae, *Dirofilaria immitis.*

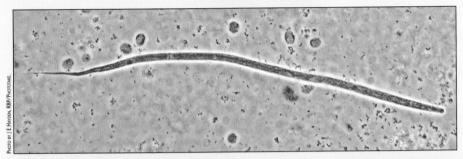

Heartworm, *Dirofilaria immitis.*

The heart of a dog infected with canine heart-worm, *Dirofilaria immitis.*

HOMEOPATHY:
an alternative to conventional medicine

"Less is Most"

Using this principle, the strength of a homeopathic remedy is measured by the number of serial dilutions that were undertaken to create it. The greater the number of serial dilutions, the greater the strength of the homeopathic remedy. The potency of a remedy that has been made by making a dilution of 1 part in 100 parts (or 1/100) is 1c or 1cH. If this remedy is subjected to a series of further dilutions, each one being 1/100, a more dilute and stronger remedy is produced. If the remedy is diluted in this way six times, it is called 6c or 6cH. A dilution of 6c is 1 part in 1,000,000,000,000. In general, higher potencies in more frequent doses are better for acute symptoms and lower potencies in more infrequent doses are more useful for chronic, long-standing problems.

CURING OUR DOGS NATURALLY

Holistic medicine means treating the whole animal as a unique, perfect living being. Generally, holistic treatments do not suppress the symptoms that the body naturally produces, as do most medications prescribed by conventional doctors and vets. Holistic methods seek to cure disease by regaining balance and harmony in the patient's environment. Some of these methods include use of nutritional therapy, herbs, flower essences, aromatherapy, acupuncture, massage, chiropractic and, of course, the most popular holistic approach, homeopathy.

Homeopathy is a theory or system of treating illness with small doses of substances which, if administered in larger quantities, would produce the symptoms that the patient already has. This approach is often described as "like cures like." Although modern veterinary medicine is geared toward the "quick fix," homeopathy relies on the belief that, given the time, the body is able to heal itself and return to its natural, healthy state.

Choosing a remedy to cure a problem in our dogs is the difficult part of homeopathy. Consult with your vet for a professional diagnosis of your dog's symptoms. Often

these symptoms require immediate conventional care. If your vet is willing and knowledgeable, you may attempt a homeopathic remedy. Be aware that cortisone prevents homeopathic remedies from working. There are hundreds of possibilities and combinations to cure many problems in dogs, from basic physical problems such as excessive shedding, fleas or other parasites, unattractive doggy odor, bad breath, upset tummy, obesity, dry, oily or dull coat, diarrhea, ear problems or eye discharge (including tears and dry or mucousy matter), to behavioral abnormalities such as fear of loud noises, habitual licking, poor appetite, excessive barking and various phobias. From alumina to zincum metallicum, the remedies span the planet and the imagination...from flowers and weeds to chemicals, insect droppings, diesel smoke and volcanic ash.

Using "Like to Treat Like"

Unlike conventional medicines that suppress symptoms, homeopathic remedies treat illnesses with small doses of substances that, if administered in larger quantities, would produce the symptoms that the patient already has. While the same homeopathic remedy can be used to treat different symptoms in different dogs, here are some interesting remedies and their uses.

Apis Mellifica
(made from honey bee venom) can be used for allergies or to reduce swelling that occurs in acutely infected kidneys.

Diesel Smoke
can be used to help control travel sickness.

Calcarea Fluorica
(made from calcium fluoride, which helps harden bone structure) can be useful in treating hard lumps in tissues.

Natrum Muriaticum
(made from common salt, sodium chloride) is useful in treating thin, thirsty dogs.

Nitricum Acidum
(made from nitric acid) is used for symptoms you would expect to see from contact with acids, such as lesions, especially where the skin joins the linings of body orifices or openings such as the lips and nostrils.

Symphytum
(made from the herb Knitbone, *Symphytum officianale*) is used to encourage bones to heal.

Urtica Urens
(made from the common stinging nettle) is used in treating painful, irritating rashes.

Recognizing a Sick Dog

Unlike colicky babies and cranky children, our canine charges cannot tell us when they are feeling ill. Therefore, there are a number of signs that owners can identify to know that their dogs are not feeling well.

Take note for physical manifestations such as:

- unusual, bad odor, including bad breath
- excessive shedding
- wax in the ears, chronic ear irritation
- oily, flaky, dull haircoat
- mucus, tearing or similar discharge in the eyes
- fleas or mites
- mucus in stool, diarrhea
- sensitivity to petting or handling
- licking at paws, scratching face, etc.

Keep an eye out for behavioral changes as well including:

- lethargy, idleness
- lack of patience or general irritability
- lack of appetite
- phobias (fear of people, loud noises, etc.)
- strange behavior, suspicion, fear
- coprophagia
- more frequent barking
- whimpering, crying

Get Well Soon

You don't need a DVM to provide good TLC to your sick or recovering dog, but you do need to pay attention to some details that normally wouldn't bother him. The following tips will aid Fido's recovery and get him back on his paws again:

- Keep his space free of irritating smells, like heavy perfumes and air fresheners.
- Rest is the best medicine! Avoid harsh lighting that will prevent your dog from sleeping. Shade him from bright sunlight during the day and dim the lights in the evening.
- Keep the noise level down. Animals are more sensitive to sound when they are sick.

- Be attentive to any necessary temperature adjustments. A dog with a fever needs a cool room and cold liquids. A bitch that is whelping or recovering from surgery will be more comfortable in a warm room, consuming warm liquids and food.
- You wouldn't send a sick child back to school early, so don't rush your dog back into a full routine until he seems absolutely ready.

Number-One Killer Disease in Dogs: CANCER

In every age, there is a word associated with a disease or plague that causes humans to shudder. In the 21st century, that word is "cancer." Just as cancer is the leading cause of death in humans, it claims nearly half the lives of dogs that die from a natural disease as well as half the dogs that die over the age of ten years.

Described as a genetic disease, cancer becomes a greater risk as the dog ages. Veterinary surgeons and dog owners have become increasingly aware of the threat of cancer to dogs. Statistics reveal that one dog in every five will develop cancer, the most common of which is skin cancer. Many cancers, including prostate, ovarian and breast cancer, can be avoided by spaying and neutering our dogs by the age of six months.

Early detection of cancer can save or extend your dog's life, so it is absolutely vital for owners to have their dogs examined by a qualified vet or oncologist immediately upon detection of any abnormality. Certain dietary guidelines have also proven to reduce the onset and spread of cancer. Foods based on fish rather than beef, due to the presence of Omega-3 fatty acids, are recommended. Other amino acids such as glutamine have significant benefits for canines, particularly those breeds that show a greater susceptibility to cancer.

Cancer management and treatments promise hope for future generations of canines. Since the disease is genetic, breeders should never breed a dog whose parents, grandparents and any related siblings have developed cancer. It is difficult to know whether to exclude an otherwise healthy dog from a breeding program as the disease does not manifest itself until the dog's senior years.

RECOGNIZE CANCER WARNING SIGNS

Since early detection can possibly rescue your dog from becoming a cancer statistic, it is essential for owners to recognise the possible signs and seek the assistance of a qualified professional.

- Abnormal bumps or lumps that continue to grow
- Bleeding or discharge from any body cavity
- Persistent stiffness or lameness
- Recurrent sores or sores that do not heal
- Inappetence
- Breathing difficulties
- Weight loss
- Bad breath or odors
- General malaise and fatigue
- Eating and swallowing problems
- Difficulty urinating and defecating

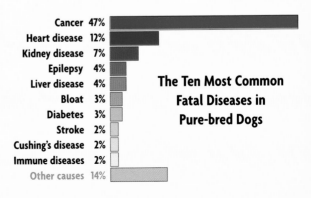

Disease	%
Cancer	47%
Heart disease	12%
Kidney disease	7%
Epilepsy	4%
Liver disease	4%
Bloat	3%
Diabetes	3%
Stroke	2%
Cushing's disease	2%
Immune diseases	2%
Other causes	14%

The Ten Most Common Fatal Diseases in Pure-bred Dogs

SPANISH WATER DOG

The term *old* is a qualitative term. For dogs, as well as for their masters, old is relative. Certainly we can all distinguish between a puppy Spanish Water Dog and an adult Spanish Water Dog—there are the obvious physical traits, such as size, appearance and facial expressions, and personality traits. Puppies and young dogs like to play with children. Children's natural exuberance is a good match for the seemingly endless energy of young dogs. They like to run, jump, chase and retrieve. When dogs grow older and cease their interaction with children, they are often thought of as being too old to keep pace with the kids. On the other hand, if a Spanish Water Dog is only exposed to people with quieter lifestyles, his life will normally be less active and the decrease in his activity level as he ages will not be as obvious.

If people live to be 100 years old, dogs live to be 20 years old. While this might seem like a good rule of thumb, it is very inaccurate. When trying to compare dog years to human years, you cannot make a generalization about all

---

GETTING OLD

The bottom line is simply that your dog is getting old when you think he is getting old because he slows down in his level of general activity, including walking, running, eating, jumping and retrieving. On the other hand, the frequency of certain activities increases, such as more sleeping, more barking and more repetition of habits like going to the door without being called when you put your coat on to leave the house.

---

dogs. Blessed with remarkable longevity, the Spanish Water Dog commonly lives to be about 14 years of age.

Dogs generally are considered physically mature at three years of age (or earlier), but can reproduce even earlier. So, generally speaking, the first three years of a dog's life are like seven times that of comparable humans. That means a 3-year-old dog is like a 21-year-old human. As the curve of comparison shows, there is no hard and fast rule for comparing dog and human ages. Small breeds tend to live longer than large breeds, some breeds' adolescent periods last longer than others' and some breeds experience rapid periods of growth. The comparison is made even more difficult, for, likewise, not all humans age at the same rate...and human females live longer than human males.

WHAT TO LOOK FOR IN SENIORS

Most vets and behaviorists use the seven-year mark as the time to consider a dog a senior, though some prefer to wait until the Spanish Water Dog is eight or nine years of age. Nevertheless, the term *senior* does not imply that the dog is geriatric and has begun to fail in mind and body. Aging is essentially a slowing process.

Humans readily admit that they feel a difference in their activity level from age 20 to 30, and then from 30 to 40, etc. By treating the seven-year-old dog as a senior, owners are able to implement certain therapeutic and preventative medical strategies with the help of their vets.

A senior-care program should include at least two veterinary visits per year and screening sessions to determine the dog's health status, as well as nutritional counseling. Vets determine the senior dog's health status through a blood smear for a complete blood count, serum chemistry profile with electrolytes, urinalysis, blood pressure check, electrocardiogram, ocular tonometry

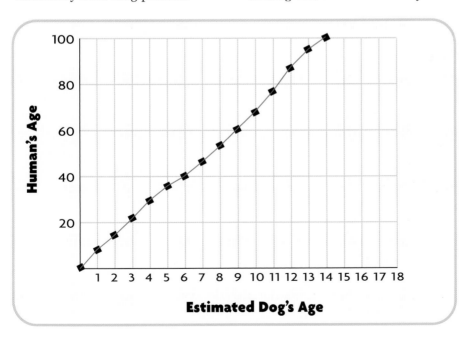

At eight years of age, this senior is still an active and attentive companion. The Spanish Water Dog is fortunate to enjoy such a long life expectancy.

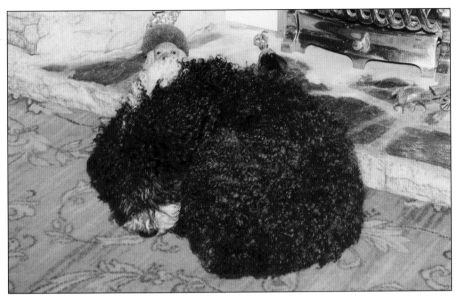

As your dog ages, he will likely sleep more and take more frequent breaks to rest.

(pressure on the eyeball) and dental prophylaxis.

Such an extensive program for senior dogs is well advised before owners start to see the obvious physical signs of aging, such as slower and inhibited movement, graying, increased sleep/nap periods and disinterest in play and other activity. This preventative program promises a longer, healthier life for the aging dog. Among the physical problems common in aging dogs are the loss of sight and hearing, arthritis, kidney and liver failure, diabetes mellitus, heart disease and Cushing's disease (a hormonal disease).

In addition to the physical manifestations discussed, there are some behavioral changes and problems related to aging dogs. Dogs suffering from hearing or vision loss, dental discomfort or arthritis can become aggressive. Likewise, the near-deaf and/or blind dog may be startled more easily and react in an unexpectedly aggressive manner. Seniors suffering from senility can become more impatient and irritable. Housesoiling accidents are associated with loss of mobility, kidney problems and loss of sphincter control as well as plaque accumulation, physiological brain changes and reactions to medications. Older dogs, just like young puppies, suffer from separation anxiety, which can lead to excessive barking, whining, housesoiling and destructive behavior. Seniors may become fearful of everyday sounds, such as vacuum cleaners, heaters, thunder and passing traffic. Some dogs have difficulty sleeping, due to discomfort, the need for frequent relief and the like.

Owners should avoid spoiling the older dog with too many fatty treats. Obesity is a common problem in older dogs and subtracts years from their lives. Keep the senior dog as trim as possible, since excessive weight puts additional stress on the body's vital organs. Some breeders recommend supplementing the diet with foods high in fiber and lower in calories. Adding fresh vegetables and marrow broth to the senior's diet makes a tasty, low-calorie, low-fat supplement. Vets also offer specialty diets for senior dogs that are worth exploring.

Your dog, as he nears his twilight years, needs your patience and good care more than ever. Never punish an older dog for an accident or abnormal behavior. For all the years of love, protection and companionship that your dog has provided, he deserves special attention and courtesies. The older dog may need to relieve himself at 3 a.m. because he can no longer "hold it" for eight hours. Older dogs may not be able to remain crated for more than two or three hours. It may be time to give up a sofa or chair to your old friend. Although he may not seem as enthusiastic about your attention and petting, he does appreciate the considerations you offer as he gets older.

Your Spanish Water Dog does not understand why his world is slowing down. Owners must make their dogs' transition into their golden years as pleasant and rewarding as possible.

AN ANCIENT ACHE

As ancient a disease as any, arthritis remains poorly explained for human and dog alike. Fossils dating back 100 million years show the deterioration caused by arthritis. Human fossils two million years old show the disease in man. The most common type of arthritis affecting dogs is known as osteoarthritis, which occurs in adult dogs before their senior years. Obesity aggravating the dog's joints has been cited as a factor in arthritis.

Rheumatoid disease destroys joint cartilage and causes arthritic joints. Pituitary dysfunctions as well as diabetes have been associated with arthritis. Vets treat arthritis variously, including aspirin, "bed rest" in the dog's crate, physical therapy and exercise, heat therapy (with a heating pad), providing soft bedding materials and treatment with corticosteroids (to reduce pain and swelling temporarily). Your vet will be able to recommend a course of action to help relieve your arthritic pal.

WHAT TO DO WHEN THE TIME COMES

You are never fully prepared to make a rational decision about putting your dog to sleep. It is very obvious that you love your Spanish Water Dog or you would not be reading this book. Putting a beloved dog to sleep is extremely difficult. It is a decision that must be made with your vet. You are usually forced to make the decision when your dog experiences one or more life-threatening symptoms that have become serious enough for you to seek veterinary help.

If the prognosis of the malady indicates that the end is near and that your beloved pet will only continue to suffer and experience no enjoyment for the balance of his life, then euthanasia is the right choice.

WHAT IS EUTHANASIA?

Euthanasia derives from the Greek, meaning *good death*. In other words, it means the planned, painless killing of a dog suffering from a painful, incurable condition, or who is so aged that he cannot walk, see, eat

"Age is in your mind," says this sprightly senior Spanish Water Dog.

or control his excretory functions. Euthanasia is usually accomplished by injection with an overdose of anesthesia or a barbiturate. Aside from the prick of the needle, the experience is usually painless.

MAKING THE DECISION

The decision to euthanize your dog is never easy. The days during which the dog becomes ill and the end occurs can be unusually stressful for you. If this is your first experience with the death of a loved one, you may need the comfort dictated by your religious beliefs. If you are the head of the family and have children, you should have

---

TALK IT OUT

The more openly your family discusses the whole stressful occurrence of the aging and eventual loss of a beloved pet, the easier it will be for you when the time comes.

involved them in the decision of putting your Spanish Water Dog to sleep. Usually your dog can be maintained on drugs for a few days in order to give you ample time to make a decision. During this time, talking with members of your family or with people who have lived through the same experience can ease the burden of your inevitable decision.

THE FINAL RESTING PLACE

Dogs can have some of the same privileges as humans. The remains of your beloved dog can be buried in a pet cemetery, which is generally expensive. Dogs who have died at home can be buried on your property in a place suitably marked with some stone or newly planted tree or bush, although this is unlawful in some countries. Alternatively, your dog can be cremated individually and the ashes returned to you. A less expensive option is mass cremation, although, of course, the ashes cannot then be returned. Vets can usually arrange the cremation on your behalf. The cost of these options should always be discussed frankly and openly with your vet.

GETTING ANOTHER DOG?

The grief of losing your beloved dog will be as lasting as the grief of losing a human friend or relative. In most cases, if your dog died of old age (if there is such a thing), he

COPING WITH LOSS

When your dog dies, you may be as upset as when a human companion passes away. You are losing your protector, your baby, your confidante and your best friend. Many people experience not only grief but also feelings of guilt and doubt as to whether they did all that they could for their pet. Allow yourself to grieve and mourn, and seek help from friends and support groups. You may also wish to consult books and websites that deal with this topic.

had slowed down considerably. Do you want a new Spanish Water Dog puppy to replace him? Or are you better off finding a more mature Spanish Water Dog, say two to three years of age, which will usually be house-trained and will have an already developed personality. In this case, you can find out if you like each other after a few hours of being together.

The decision is, of course, your own. Do you want another Spanish Water Dog or perhaps a different breed so as to avoid comparison with your beloved friend? Most people usually buy the same breed because they know (and love) the characteristics of that breed. Then, too, they may know people who have the same breed and perhaps they are lucky enough that a breeder they know and respect expects a litter soon.

SHOWING YOUR
SPANISH WATER DOG

When you purchase your Spanish Water Dog, you will make it clear to the breeder whether you want one just as a lovable companion and pet, or if you hope to be buying a Spanish Water Dog with show prospects. No reputable breeder will sell you a young puppy and tell you that it is *definitely* of show quality, for so much can go wrong during the early months of a puppy's development. If you plan to show, what you will hopefully have acquired is a puppy with "show potential."

To the novice, exhibiting a Spanish Water Dog in the show

Competing in a dog show under the auspices of the Fédération Cynologique Internationale, this Spanish Water Dog is being gaited in the ring by his handler.

A Group placement at an international show is a major accomplishment for the Spanish Water Dog. The breed is gaining a stronghold outside Spain and has won major awards at FCI shows.

ring may look easy, but it takes a lot of hard work and devotion to do top winning at prestigious conformation shows, not to mention a little luck too!

The first concept that the canine novice learns when watching a dog show is that each dog first competes against members of his own breed. Once the judge has selected the best member of each breed (Best of Breed), provided that the show is judged on a Group system, that

chosen dog will compete with other dogs in his group. Finally, the dogs chosen first in each group will compete for Best in Show.

The second concept that you must understand is that the dogs are not actually compared against one another. The judge compares each dog against his breed standard. While some early breed standards were indeed based on specific dogs that were famous or popular, many dedicated enthusiasts say that a perfect specimen, as described in the standard, has never walked into a show ring, has never been bred and, to the woe of dog breeders around the globe, does not exist. Breeders attempt to get as close to this ideal as possible with every litter, but theoretically the "perfect" dog is so elusive that it is impossible. (And if the "perfect" dog were born, breeders and judges probably would never agree that it was indeed "perfect.")

If you are interested in exploring the world of dog showing, your best bet is to join your local breed club or the national, or parent, club. These clubs often host both regional and national specialties, shows only for Spanish Water Dogs, which can include conformation as well as obedience trials. Even if you have no intention of competing with your Spanish Water Dog, a specialty is like a festival for lovers of the breed who congregate to share their favorite topic: Spanish Water Dogs! Clubs also send out newsletters, and some organize training days and seminars in order that people may learn more about their chosen breed.

To locate the breed club closest to you, contact the national kennel club [in the US, the American Rare Breed Association (ARBA), the United Kennel Club (UKC) or the National Kennel Club (NKC) or the breed's parent club, the Spanish Water Dog Association of America (SWDAA)]. These clubs furnish the rules and regulations for all of these events plus general dog registration and other basic requirements of dog ownership.

If your Spanish Water Dog is of age and registered, you can enter him in a dog show where the breed is offered classes. Only unaltered dogs can be entered in a dog show, so if you have spayed or neutered your Spanish Water Dog, your dog cannot compete in conformation shows. The reason for this is simple. Dog shows are the main forum to prove which representatives in a breed are worthy of being bred. Only dogs that have achieved championships— the recognized "seal of approval" for quality in pure-bred dogs—should be bred. Altered dogs, however, can participate in other events such

SHOW-RING ETIQUETTE
Just as with anything else, there is a certain etiquette to the show ring that can only be learned through experience. Showing your dog can be quite intimidating to you as a novice when it seems as if everyone else knows what he is doing. You can familiarize yourself with ring procedure beforehand by taking showing classes to prepare you and your dog for conformation showing and by talking with experienced handlers. When you are in the ring, it is very important to pay attention and listen to the instructions you are given by the judge about where to move your dog. Remember, even the most skilled handlers had to start somewhere. Keep it up and you too will become a proficient handler as you gain practice and experience.

as obedience trials, agility trials, herding trials, water dog events, etc.

Before you actually step into the ring, you would be well advised to sit back and observe the judge's ring procedure. If it is your first time in the ring, do not be over-anxious and run to the front of the line. It is much better to stand back and study how the exhibitor in front of you is performing. The judge asks each handler to stand, or "stack," the dog, hopefully showing the dog off to his best advantage. The judge will observe the dog from a distance and from different angles, and approach the dog to check his teeth, overall structure, alertness and muscle tone, as well as consider how well the dog "conforms" to the standard. Most

importantly, the judge will have the exhibitor move the dog around the ring in some pattern that he should specify (another advantage to not going first, but always listen since some judges change their directions—and the judge is always right!). Finally, the judge will give the dog one last look before moving on to the next exhibitor.

If you are not in the top four in your class at your first show, do not be discouraged. Be patient and consistent, and you may eventually find yourself in a winning line-up. Remember that the winners were once in your shoes and have devoted many hours and much money to earn the placement. If you find that your dog is losing every time and never getting a nod, it may be time to consider a different dog sport or to just enjoy your Spanish Water Dog as a pet. Clubs offer other events, such as agility, tracking, obedience, instinct tests and more, which may be of interest to the owner of a well-trained Spanish Water Dog.

INFORMATION ON CLUBS

You can get information about dog shows from the national kennel clubs:

American Kennel Club
5580 Centerview Dr.,
Raleigh, NC 27606-3390
www.akc.org

United Kennel Club
100 E. Kilgore Road,
Kalamazoo, MI 49002
www.ukcdogs.com

American Rare Breed Association
9921 Frank Tippett Road,
Cheltenham, MD 20623
www.arba.org

Fédération Cynologique Internationale
14, rue Leopold II, B-6530 Thuin, Belgium
www.fci.be

OBEDIENCE TRIALS

Obedience trials in the US trace back to the early 1930s when organized obedience training was developed to demonstrate how well dog and owner could work together. The pioneer of obedience trials is Mrs. Helen Whitehouse Walker, a Standard Poodle fancier, who designed a series of exercises after the Associated Sheep, Police Army Dog Society of Great Britain. Since the days of Mrs. Walker, obedience trials have grown by leaps and bounds, and today there are over 2,000 trials held in the US every year, with more than 100,000 dogs competing. Any registered dog can enter an obedience trial, regardless of conformational disqualifications or neutering.

Obedience trials are divided into three levels of progressive difficulty. At the first level, the Novice, dogs compete for the title Companion Dog (CD); at the intermediate level, the Open, dogs compete for the title Companion Dog Excellent (CDX); and at the advanced level, the Utility, dogs compete for the title Utility Dog (UD). Classes are sub-divided into "A" (for beginners) and "B" (for more experienced handlers). A perfect score at any level is 200, and a dog must score 170 or better to earn a "leg," of which three are needed to earn the title. To earn points, the dog must score more than 50% of the available points in each exercise; the possible points range from 20 to 40.

Each level consists of a different set of exercises. In the Novice level, the dog must heel on- and off-lead, come, long sit, long down and stand for examination. These skills are the basic ones required for a well-behaved "Companion Dog." The Open level requires that the dog perform the same exercises above but without a leash for extended lengths of time, as well as retrieve a dumbbell, broad jump and drop on recall. In the Utility level, dogs must perform ten difficult exercises, including scent discrimination, hand signals for basic commands, directed jump and directed retrieve.

Once a dog has earned the UD title, he can compete with other proven obedience dogs for the coveted title of Utility Dog Excellent (UDX), which requires that the dog win "legs" in ten shows. Utility Dogs who earn "legs" in Open B and Utility B earn points toward their Obedience Trial Champion title. In 1977, the title Obedience Trial Champion (OTCh.) was established by the American Kennel Club (AKC). To become an OTCh., a dog needs to earn 100 points, which requires three first places in Open B and Utility under three different judges.

WATER TESTS

Most countries offer some type of water test for the Spanish Water Dog and other water breeds, which include all of the retriever breeds as well as the Portuguese Water Dog, Barbet and other such aquatic wonders.

AGILITY TRIALS

Having had its origins in the UK back in 1977, AKC agility had its official beginning in the US in August 1994, when the first licensed agility trials were held. The AKC allows all registered breeds (including Miscellaneous Class breeds) to participate, providing the dog is 12 months of age or older. Agility is designed so that the handler demonstrates how well the dog can work at his side. The handler directs his dog over an obstacle course that includes jumps (such as those used in obedience trials), as well as tires, the dog walk, weave poles, pipe tunnels, collapsed tunnels, etc. While working his way through the course, the dog must keep one eye and ear on the handler and the rest of his body on the course. The handler gives verbal and hand signals to guide the dog through the course.

The first organization to promote agility trials in the US was the United States Dog Agility Association, Inc. (USDAA), which was established in 1986 and spawned numerous member clubs around the country. Both the USDAA and the AKC offer titles to winning dogs. Three titles are available through the USDAA: Agility Dog (AD), Advanced Agility Dog (AAD) and Master Agility Dog (MAD). The AKC offers Novice Agility (NA), Open Agility (OA), Agility Excellent (AX) and Master Agility Excellent (MX). Beyond these four AKC titles, dogs can win additional ones in "jumper" classes, Jumpers with Weave Novice (NAJ), Open (OAJ) and Excellent (MXJ), which lead to the ultimate title(s): MACH, Master Agility Champion. Dogs can continue to add number designations to the MACH titles, indicating how many times the dog has met the MACH requirements, such as MACH1, MACH2, and so forth.

Agility is great fun for dog and owner with many rewards for everyone involved. Interested owners should join a training club that has obstacles and experienced agility handlers who can introduce you and your dog to the "ropes" (and tires, tunnels, etc.).

PRACTICE AT HOME

If you have decided to show your dog, you must train him to gait around the ring by your side at the correct pace and pattern, and to tolerate being handled and examined by the judge. Most breeds require complete dentition, all breeds require a particular bite (scissors, level or undershot) and all males must have two apparently normal testicles fully descended into the scrotum. Enlist family and friends to hold mock trials in your yard to prepare your future champion!

HERDING TESTS AND TRIALS

Since the first sheepdog trials recorded in the late 19th century in Wales, the practice of herding trials has grown tremendously around the world. The first trial began as a friendly match to see which farmer's dog was the best at moving sheep. Today the sport is more organized than in those early days, and all herding breeds can earn titles at these fun and competitive events.

The AKC offers herding trials and tests to any recognized herding dog that is nine months of age or older. The handler is expected to direct the dog to herd various livestock, including sheep, ducks, goats and cattle. There are two titles for herding tests: Herding Tested (HT) and Pre-Trial Tested (PT). If the dog shows a basic innate ability, it is awarded a HT title; the PT title is awarded to a dog that can herd a small herd of livestock through a basic course.

In herding trials, there are four titles awarded: Herding Started (HS), Herding Intermediate (HI), Herding Excellent (HX) and Herding Champion (HCh.), the latter of which is awarded to a dog who has demonstrated mastery of herding in the most demanding of circumstances. Like shows, herding trials are judged against a set of standards as well as other dogs.

FÉDÉRATION CYNOLOGIQUE INTERNATIONALE

Established in 1911, the Fédération Cynologique Internationale (FCI) represents the "world kennel club." This international body brings uniformity to the breeding, judging and showing of pure-bred dogs. Although the FCI originally included only 5 European nations: France, Germany, Austria, the Netherlands and Belgium (which remains its headquarters), the organization today embraces nations on 6 continents and recognizes well over 300 breeds of pure-bred dog.

The FCI sponsors both national and international shows. The hosting country determines the judging system and breed

A GENTLEMAN'S SPORT

Whether or not your dog wins top honors, showing is a pleasant social event. Sometimes, one may meet a troublemaker or nasty exhibitor, but these people should be ignored and forgotten. In the extremely rare case that someone threatens or harasses you or your dog, you can lodge a complaint with the hosting kennel club. This should be done with extreme prudence. Complaints are investigated seriously and should never be filed on a whim.

standards are always based on the breed's country of origin. Dogs from every country can participate in these impressive canine spectacles, the largest of which is the World Dog Show, hosted in a different country each year.

There are three titles attainable through the FCI: the International Champion, which is the most prestigious; the International Beauty Champion, which is based on aptitude certificates in different countries; and the International Trial Champion, which is based on achievement in obedience trials in different countries. An FCI title requires a dog to win three CACs

(*Certificats d'Aptitude au Championnat*) at regional or club shows under three different judges who are breed specialists. The title of International Champion is gained by winning four CACIBs (*Certificats d'Aptitude au Championnat International de Beauté*), which are offered only at international shows, with at least a one-year lapse between the first and fourth award.

The FCI is divided into ten groups, and the Spanish Water Dog is exhibited in Group 8 for Retrievers, Flushers and Water Dogs. At the World Dog Show, the following classes are offered for each breed: Puppy Class (6–9 months), Junior Class (9–18 months), Open Class (15 months or older) and Champion Class. A dog can be awarded a classification of Excellent, Very Good, Good, Sufficient and Not Sufficient. Puppies can be awarded classifications of Very Promising, Promising or Not Promising. Four placements are made in each class. After all classes are judged, a Best of Breed is selected. Other special groups and classes may also be shown. Each exhibitor showing a dog receives a written evaluation from the judge.

Besides the World Dog Show and other all-breed shows, you can exhibit your dog at specialty shows held by different breed clubs. Specialty shows may have their own regulations.

BEHAVIOR OF YOUR
SPANISH WATER DOG

As a Spanish Water Dog owner, you have selected your dog so that you and your loved ones can have a companion, a protector, a swimming buddy and a four-legged family member. You invest time, money and effort to care for and train the family's new charge. Of course, this chosen canine behaves perfectly! Well, perfectly like a *dog*.

THINK LIKE A DOG

Dogs do not think like humans, nor do humans think like dogs, though we try. Unfortunately, a dog is incapable of comprehending how humans think, so the responsibility falls on the owner to adopt a viable canine mindset. Dogs cannot rationalize, and they exist in the present moment. Many a dog owner makes the mistake in training of thinking that he can reprimand his dog for something that the dog did a while ago. Basically, you cannot even reprimand a dog for something he did 20 seconds ago! Either catch him in the act or forget it! It is a waste of your and your dog's time—in his mind, you are reprimanding him for whatever he is doing at that moment.

The following behavioral problems represent some which owners most commonly encounter. Every dog is unique and every situation is unique. No author could purport for you to

It's no small task to get inside the head of the Spanish Water Dog. This is a quick-minded working animal, capable of making decisions on his own!

solve your Spanish Water Dog's problems simply by reading a chapter. Here we outline some basic "dogspeak" so that owners' chances of solving behavioral problems are increased.

Discuss bad habits with your vet and he can recommend a behavioral specialist to consult in appropriate cases. Since behavioral abnormalities are the main reason for owners' abandoning their pets, we hope that you will make a valiant effort to solve your Spanish Water Dog's problems. Patience and understanding are virtues that must dwell in every pet-loving household.

AGGRESSION
This is a problem that concerns all responsible dog owners, even owners of dogs that are not aggressive by nature. Aggression can be a very big problem in dogs, and, when not controlled, always becomes dangerous. An aggressive dog, no matter the size, may lunge at, bite or even attack a person or another dog. Aggressive behavior is not to be tolerated. It is more than just inappropriate behavior; it is painful for a family to watch their dog become unpredictable in his behavior to the point where they are afraid of him. While not all aggressive behaviors are dangerous, growling, baring teeth, etc., can be frightening. It is important to ascertain why the

dog is acting in this manner. Aggression is a display of dominance, and the dog should not have the dominant role in his pack, which is, in this case, your family.

It is important not to challenge an aggressive dog, as this could provoke an attack. Observe your Spanish Water Dog's body language. Does he make direct eye contact and stare? Does he try to make himself as large as possible: ears pricked, chest out, tail erect? Height and size signify authority in a dog pack—being taller or above another dog literally means that he is "above" in social status. These body signals tell you that your Spanish Water Dog thinks he is in charge, a problem that needs to be addressed. An aggressive dog is unpredictable; you never know when he is going to strike and what he is going to do. You cannot understand why a dog that is playful one minute is growling the next.

Fear is a common cause of

DOMINANT AGGRESSION
Never allow your puppy to growl at you or bare his tiny teeth. Such behavior is dominant and aggressive. If not corrected, the dog will repeat the behavior, which will become more threatening as he grows larger and will eventually lead to biting.

aggression in dogs. Perhaps your Spanish Water Dog had a negative experience as a puppy, which causes him to be fearful when a similar situation presents itself later in life. The dog may act aggressively in order to protect himself from whatever is making him afraid. It is not always easy to determine what is making your dog fearful, but if you can isolate what brings out the fear reaction, you can help the dog to get over it.

Supervise your Spanish Water Dog's interactions with people and other dogs, and praise the dog when it goes well. If he starts to act aggressively in a situation, correct him and remove him from the situation. Do not let people approach the dog and start petting him without your express permission. That way, you can have the dog sit to accept petting, and praise him when he behaves properly. You are focusing on praise and on modifying his behavior by rewarding him when he acts appropriately. By being gentle and by supervising his interactions, you are showing him that there is no need to be afraid or defensive.

BARKING
Spanish Water Dogs are vocally gifted, often barking happily during playtime, and they use their barks to alert their owners to changes in their environment. Some puppies tend to be rather

DOG TALK
Deciphering your dog's barks is very similar to understanding a baby's cries: there is a different cry for eating, sleeping, potty needs, etc. Your dog talks to you not only through howls and groans but also through his body language. Baring teeth, staring and inflating the chest are all threatening gestures. If a dog greets you by licking his nose, turning his head or yawning, these are friendly, peacemaking gestures.

vocal, so owners must determine when their Spanish Water Dog's barking is desired and useful, and when it is just showing off and noisy.

For example, if an intruder came into your home in the middle of the night and your Spanish Water Dog barked a warning, wouldn't you be pleased? You would probably deem your dog a hero, a wonderful guardian and protector of the home. On the other hand, if a friend drops by unexpectedly, rings the doorbell and is greeted with a sudden sharp bark, you would probably be annoyed at the dog. But in reality, isn't this just the same behavior? The dog does not know any better. Unless he sees who is at the door and it is someone whom he knows, he will bark as a means of vocalizing that his (and your) territory is being threatened. While your friend is not posing a threat, it is all the same to the dog. Barking is his means of letting you know that there is an intrusion, whether friend or foe, on your property. This type of barking is instinctive and should not be discouraged.

Excessive habitual barking, however, is a problem that should be corrected early on. As your Spanish Water Dog grows up, you will be able to tell when his barking is purposeful and when it is for no reason. You will become able to distinguish your dog's different barks and their meanings. For example, the bark when someone comes to the door will be different from the bark when he is excited to see you. It is similar to a person's tone of voice, except that the dog has to rely totally on tone of voice because he does not have the benefit of using words. An incessant barker will be evident at an early age.

There are some things that encourage a dog to bark. For example, if your dog barks non-stop for a few minutes and you give him a treat to quiet him, he believes that you are rewarding him for barking. He will associate barking with getting a treat and will keep doing it until he is rewarded. On the other hand, if you give him a command such as "Quiet" and praise him after he

> **HE'S PROTECTING YOU**
> Barking is your dog's way of protecting you. If he barks at a stranger walking past your house, a moving car or a fleeing cat, he is merely exercising his responsibility to protect his pack (YOU) and territory from a perceived intruder. Since the "intruder" usually keeps going, the dog thinks his barking chased it away and he feels fulfilled. This behavior leads your overly vocal friend to believe that he is the "dog in charge."

has stopped barking for a few seconds, he will get the idea that being "quiet" is what you want him to do.

SEXUAL BEHAVIOR
Dogs exhibit certain sexual behaviors that may have influenced your choice of male or female when you first purchased your Spanish Water Dog. To a certain extent, spaying/neutering will eliminate these behaviors, but if you are purchasing a dog from whom you wish to breed, you should be aware of what you will have to deal with throughout the dog's life.

Female dogs usually have two estruses per year, with each season lasting about three weeks. These are the only times in which a female dog will mate, and she usually will not allow this until the second week of the cycle, although this varies from bitch to bitch. If not bred during the heat cycle, it is not uncommon for a bitch to experience a false pregnancy, in which her mammary glands swell and she exhibits maternal tendencies toward toys or other objects.

With male dogs, owners must be aware that whole dogs (dogs who are not neutered) have the natural inclination to mark their territory. Males mark their territory by spraying small amounts of urine as they lift their legs in a macho ritual. Marking can occur both outdoors in the garden and around the neighborhood as well as indoors on furniture legs, curtains and the sofa. Such behavior can be very frustrating for the owner; early training is strongly urged before the "urge" strikes your dog. Neutering the male at an appropriate early age can solve this problem before it becomes a habit.

Other problems associated with males are wandering and mounting. Both of these habits, of course, belong to the unneutered dog, whose sexual drive leads him away from home in search of the bitch in heat. Males will mount females in heat, as well as any other dog, male or female, that happens to catch their fancy. Other possible mounting partners include his owner, the furniture, guests to the home and strangers on the street. Discourage such behavior early on.

Owners must further recognize that mounting is not merely a sexual expression but also one of dominance, seen in males and females alike. Be consistent and be persistent, and you will find that you can "move mounters."

SEPARATION ANXIETY
Recognized by behaviorists as the most common form of stress for dogs, separation anxiety can also lead to destructive behaviors in your dog. It's more than your Spanish Water Dog's howling his displeasure at your leaving the house and his being left alone. This is a normal reaction, no different from the child who cries

Male dogs are infamously more difficult to house-train, mainly because they are more fixated on their scatological functions. Lifting his leg, this macho, *guapo* Perro is leaving his calling card for passing *muchachas.*

as his mother leaves him on the first day at school. Separation anxiety is more serious. In fact, if you are constantly with your dog, he will come to expect you with him all of the time, making it even more traumatic for him when you are not there.

Obviously, you enjoy spending time with your dog, and he thrives on your love and attention. However, it should not become a dependent relationship in which he is heartbroken without you. This broken heart can also bring on destructive behavior as well as loss of appetite, depression and lack of interest in play and interaction. Canine behaviorists have been spending much time and energy to help owners better understand the significance of this stressful condition.

One thing you can do to minimize separation anxiety is to make your entrances and exits as low-key as possible. Do not give your dog a long drawn-out goodbye, and do not lavish him with hugs and kisses when you return. This is giving in to the attention that he craves, and it will only make him miss it more when you are away. Another thing you can try is to give your dog a treat when you leave; this not only will keep him occupied and keep his mind off the fact that you have just left but also will help him associate your leaving with a pleasant experience.

SET AN EXAMPLE
Never scream, shout, jump or run about if you want your dog to stay calm. You set the example for your dog's behavior in most circumstances. Learn from your dog's reaction to your behavior and act accordingly.

DIGGING
Digging, which is seen as a destructive behavior to humans, is actually quite a natural behavior in dogs. Although terriers (the "earth dogs") are most associated with the digging, any dog's desire to dig can be irrepressible and most frustrating to his owners. Spanish Water Dogs can develop destructive digging habits if left for hours on end without "jobs" to do. Boredom is usually to blame, as opposed to the need to escape or the pursuit of vermin.

A dog feels useful when he digs. Thus, when digging occurs in your lawn, it is actually a normal behavior redirected into something the dog can do in his everyday life. In the wild, a dog would be actively seeking food, making his own shelter, etc. He would be using his paws in a purposeful manner for his survival. Since you provide him with food and shelter, he has no need to use his paws for these purposes, and so the energy that he would be using may manifest itself in the form of little holes all over your yard and flower beds.

To eliminate boredom digging, provide the dog with adequate play and exercise so that his mind and paws are occupied, and so that he feels as if he is doing something useful. Digging is easiest to control if it is stopped as soon as possible, but it is often hard to catch a dog in the act. If your dog is a compulsive digger and is not easily distracted by other activities, you can designate an area on your property where he is allowed to dig. If you catch him digging in an off-limits area of the yard, immediately bring him to the approved area and praise him for digging there. Keep a close eye on him so that you can catch him in the act—that is the only way to make him understand what is permitted and what is not. If you take him to a hole that he dug an hour ago and tell him "No," he will understand that you are not fond of holes, dirt or flowers. If you catch him while he is stifle-deep in your tulips, that is when he will get your message.

JUMPING UP

No matter how friendly the greeting, your Spanish Water Dog's jumping up on a visitor to your home should be discouraged early on. As with all problem behaviors, it is advised that you

NO JUMPING

Stop a dog from jumping up before he jumps. If he is getting ready to jump onto you, simply walk away. If he jumps up on you before you can turn away, lift your knee so that it bumps him in the chest. Do not be forceful. Your dog soon will realize that jumping up is not a productive way of getting attention.

extinguish this behavior while the Spanish Water Dog is still a pup. Pick a command such as "Off" (avoid using "Down" since you will use that for the dog to lie down) and tell him "Off" when he jumps up. Place him on the ground on all fours and have him sit, praising him the whole time. Always lavish him with praise and petting when he is in the sit position. In this way, you can give him a warm affectionate greeting, let him know that you are as excited to see him as he is to see you and instill good manners at the same time!

CHEWING

The national canine pastime is chewing, even though most Spanish Water Dogs aren't overly aggressive chewers. Nevertheless, from time to time, every dog loves to sink his "canines" into a tasty bone or toy! Dogs need to chew, to massage their gums, to make their new teeth feel better and to exercise their jaws. This is a natural behavior that is deeply embedded in all things canine.

Your role as owner is not to stop the dog's chewing, but rather to redirect it to positive, chew-worthy objects. Be an informed owner and purchase top-quality chew toys, like strong nylon bones, that will not splinter. Be sure that the objects are safe and durable, since your

dog's safety is at risk. Again, the owner is responsible for ensuring a dog-proof environment.

The best answer is prevention; that is, put your shoes, coat and other tasty objects in their proper places (out of the reach of the growing canine mouth). Direct puppies to their toys whenever you see them "tasting" the furniture legs or the pant leg of a guest. Make a loud noise to attract the pup's attention and immediately escort him to his chew toy and engage him with the toy for at least four minutes, praising and encouraging him all the while. An array of safe, interesting chew toys will keep your dog's mind and teeth occupied and distracted from chewing on things he shouldn't.

FOOD STEALING

Is your dog devising ways of stealing food from your coffee table or kitchen counter? If so, you must answer the following questions: Is your Spanish Water Dog hungry, or is he "constantly famished" like many dogs seem to be? Face it, some dogs are more food-motivated than others are. They are totally obsessed by the smell of food and can only think of their next meal. Food stealing is terrific fun and always yields a great reward—FOOD, glorious food.

Your goal as an owner, therefore, is to be sensible about

Milk and cookies are favorites of every domesticated dog! Do not allow you dog to indulge in sugary human foods, or he will quickly learn to help himself to the dinner table and pantry.

where food is placed in the home and to reprimand your dog whenever he is caught in the act of stealing. But remember, only reprimand your dog if you actually see him stealing, not later when the crime is discovered; that will be of no use at all and will only confuse him.

BEGGING

Just like food stealing, begging is a favorite pastime of hungry puppies! It achieves that same terrific result—FOOD! Dogs quickly learn that their owners keep the "good food" for themselves, and that we humans do not dine on dry food alone. Begging is a conditioned response related to a specific stimulus, time and place. The sounds of the kitchen, cans and bottles opening, crinkling bags, the smell of food in preparation, etc., will excite the dog, and soon the paws will be in the air!

Here is the solution to stopping this behavior: Never give in to a beggar! You are rewarding the dog for sitting pretty, jumping up, whining and rubbing his nose into you by giving him food. By ignoring the dog, you will (eventually) force the behavior into extinction. Note that the behavior is likely to get worse before it disappears, so be sure there are not any "softies" in the family who will give in to "Oliverito" every time he whimpers "More, please."

INDEX

My Spanish Water Dog

Dog's Name _____

Date _____ Photographer _____